BEST OF THE BEST PRESENTS

the complete

LOW-CARB

cookbook

BEST OF THE BEST PRESENTS

the complete

LOW-CARB

cookbook

GEORGE STELLA

WITH CHRISTIAN STELLA

QUAIL RIDGE PRESS

Preserving America's Food Heritage

Copyright ©2014 by George Stella

Published by Quail Ridge Press
www.quailridge.com

All rights reserved.
No part of this book may be reproduced in any manner, except for
brief quotations in critical articles or reviews, without permission.

First printing, April 2014 • Second, May 2014 • Third, January 2015
Fourth, March 2015 • Fifth, July 2015 • Sixth, October 2015 • Seventh, September 2016

Book Design and Food Photography by Christian and Elise Stella

---

Library of Congress Cataloging-in-Publication Data

Stella, George, author.
Best of the best presents the complete low-carb cookbook/George Stella.
—First edition.
    pages cm
Includes index.
ISBN 978-1-934193-96-9
1. Low-carbohydrate diet--Recipes. I. Title. II. Title: Complete low-carb
    cookbook.
RM237.73.S739 2014
641.5'6383--dc23   2014000780

This book is not meant to dispense medical advice. Please consult your doctor before making any dramatic changes to the way you eat.

Nutritional analysis provided on each recipe is meant only as a reference and has been compiled to best of our ability using nutritional analysis software. Due to differences in sizes, brands, and types of ingredients, your calculations may vary. Calories have been rounded to the nearest 5 and all other amounts were rounded to the nearest .5 of a gram.

Front cover: Chicken Marsala, page 89 • Stella-Style Cheesecake, page 205

Back cover: Grilled Eggplant Caprese Salad, page 59 • Mixed Berry Muffins, page 29 • Pork Tenderloin with Mustard Gravy, page 127

ISBN 978-1-934193-96-9
Printed in the United States of America

QUAIL RIDGE PRESS
P. O. Box 123 • Brandon, MS 39043 • 1800-343-1583
info@quailridge.com • www.quailridge.com

CONTENTS

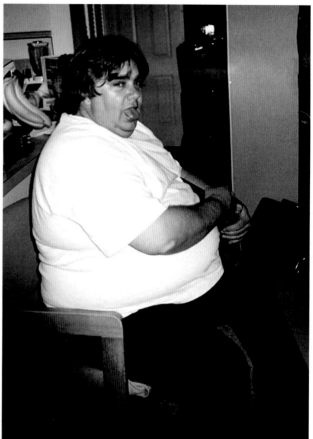

George Stella and family, before and after they lost more than 550 pounds.

Introduction

My name is George Stella and I've been living a low-carb lifestyle for nearly fifteen years. This is my sixth cookbook on the subject, but living this lifestyle has me so energized that I still feel I have more to say—and more importantly—more to cook!

Each time I set out to write a new cookbook, I ask myself how I can make things better, more *complete*. As a chef for over thirty years, I know how to cook, but it's the teaching that I've had to learn. Putting what happens in the kitchen into words was not always easy for me. Finishing a book and feeling as if I'd said all that needed to be said, and included all that needed to be included has not always been the case. For me, writing a cookbook has to be the perfect balance between the knowledge afforded to me over thirty years of being a chef, and fifteen years of living low-carb. It's a whole lot to *say*, and a whole lot to *teach*, but I truly feel this is the most *complete* book I've ever written. No, I didn't just call it *The Complete Low-Carb Cookbook* because I thought it was a catchy title!

Fifteen years ago, I weighed 467 pounds. I was sick, very sick. I had congestive heart failure, sleep apnea, and was in and out of a wheelchair. I'd had a heart attack and had to have fluid drained from my heart many, many years before—when I was still young, and when I weighed far less. Gaining as much weight as I had since my first heart attack, now weighing 467 pounds, I was just waiting to have a *second* heart attack. My doctor said it was inevitable. In fact, my doctor said that I was in such poor health in so many ways that *death* was inevitable. He was a very frank

guy, and looking back now, I need to thank him. When he told me I was going to die, something finally clicked.

My family's weight had also spiraled out of control. We were unhealthy physically and unhealthy for each other mentally, enabling one another to make poor choices. My wife Rachel, who had never had a weight problem previously, had resigned to living in a "fat family," and put on 75 pounds in only a few short years. My son Anthony was up and down over the years, eventually bordering on obese by the time he hit high school. My son Christian had been obese since the age of four. With severe asthma, Christian was in and out of hospitals his entire life, and by the age of 15, he weighed over 300 pounds. He was not just on his way to following in my footsteps; Christian already had followed in my footsteps.

When we first heard about low-carb "diets," it was in the form of a book by Dr. Atkins. With our whole family's health in jeopardy, we were willing to try anything—but with a real addiction to food, trying to lose weight was going to be easier said than done.

The beauty of a low-carb lifestyle ("diet" is a dirty word) is that you do not need to feel restricted from eating anything other than carbohydrates. As a society, we are bombarded by carbohydrates everywhere we turn and in nearly every processed food. While we

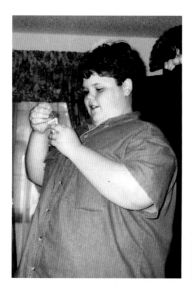

may have considered ourselves "addicted" to food, our addiction to carbohydrates was all that needed to be broken. Like anything, removing carbs from your diet (there's that word again!) is not easy at first, especially if you do not have a good support system. We started this lifestyle when very few recipes or cookbooks on low-carb even existed, and we had to work to not only figure out what would work for our weight loss, but how to cook it—and most importantly, how to reinvent all of our favorite dishes without carbohydrates.

Whether you are just starting out on a low-carb lifestyle, or have been living one for years, you can make this book your support system in the kitchen—the support system we wish we had had when we started down our journey to a healthier life. We've spent fifteen years developing recipes using naturally low-carb fresh foods, and preparing these recipes each and every day. Each time we make one of our recipes, it gets a little closer to low-carb perfection. Once a recipe is perfect, well, it has gone into the very book you are holding!

Once we stopped relying on fast food and quick-fix processed and packaged foods, once we took all of that junk out of our minds and out of our lives, we underwent a spectacular transformation in less than three years! We had not only broken our addiction to carbs,

but learned to love *real* food again, and we lost weight doing it. A lot of weight.

Though we jumped into low-carb mostly skeptical, when the weight started coming off, we knew that low-carb didn't just "work," it worked extremely well, and in a way that we didn't have to feel like we were going hungry. We weren't just eating better nutritionally, we were eating better overall—cooking and eating restaurant-quality meals that I had not prepared since my health had taken me out of my career as a chef.

All told, my family lost a total of more than 550 pounds. After personally losing 265 pounds, I proved my doctor wrong, and have been very much alive for fifteen years. Rachel lost 75 pounds and went down to the same weight she was in high school. Anthony lost 75 pounds and Christian dropped over 160 pounds (more than half of his weight) before his 18th birthday. Most importantly, we were healthy. My sons were healthy for the first time in their entire lives.

I was also a professional chef again, back to work in restaurant kitchens for the first time in a decade. But my time back as a chef on the line was very short lived, as word of our family's amazing story, and the delicious recipes we ate while creating that story got out. Within a year of losing the weight, we were featured in magazines and countless television shows. Most importantly, I had my own show on Food Network called *Low Carb and Lovin' It*. Food Network taught me a lot about how to *teach* others, how to share the amazing recipes we'd created in an easy-to-follow way. As we maintained our weight, the stories of our fans losing weight encouraged us to keep going, and to keep sharing our story with as many people that will listen.

How Low-Carb Works

Assuming you purchased this book to live a healthier lifestyle, I'd like to say that I've been on the other side of the relationship between you (the reader) and myself. I was once 467 pounds, flipping through a dense book of text by Dr. Atkins, and confused by how to make sense of it. What we eat is prepared in the kitchen, and I feel we can learn a lot more through cooking than reading. As a chef, that's what I know and all I've ever claimed to know—cooking. I'll do my best to summarize how low-carb works, but know that I'm not the person to explain *why* it works. I am not a doctor, and the real specifics of what happens inside the body should be left to a doctor to explain. Dr. Atkins and other doctors have written entire 500-page books on the subject, and there are countless studies available on the Internet to further explore the effectiveness of low-carb.

The concept of low-carb eating is quite simple. Our body can burn either carbohydrates or fat to get the energy it needs; however, it prefers carbohydrates if it is given them. When eating a diet full of carbohydrates, the body burns the carbs that it needs to get through the day, and then it converts the remaining carbohydrates into stored fat in case there is ever a time when your body needs excess fat to survive. This is why overeating leads to weight gain—the body is designed to convert food into fat and store it in the event you are ever without food, much like bears storing fat for hibernation in the winter.

Because your body has every ability to create energy from *fat*, when you do not supply it with *carbohydrates*, it creates energy from fat, and you go into a constant fat-burning state known as "ketosis." Not only do you burn the fat that you eat, but you also burn your reserved fat to get you through the day. It is hard for most people to grasp why you can eat higher fat foods on low-carb, but this is exactly why—your body is burning it right off.

Going into the "ketosis" state is a pretty simple thing to do; you just stop eating processed carbohydrates. Staying in a state of "*ketosis*" is the most important thing I can stress. Cheating on a low-carb lifestyle will immediately switch your body out of "*ketosis*" and back to burning carbohydrates instead of fat.

Studies have proven that eating fat on a low-carb lifestyle does not raise your cholesterol. My own family's cholesterol went way, way down once we started eating low-carb, but you will not get those benefits if you cheat and eat processed high-carb foods once a day. Studies have proven time and time again that low-carb actually works, but you've got to commit to it! It truly is a lifestyle.

All of that said, eating more fresh and natural foods can't hurt, regardless of whether you are living a low-carb lifestyle or not! We surround ourselves with fresh foods that are naturally low-carb, because that is what worked for us, and quite frankly, we don't like to get caught up in why it works for us, we just know that it does and that we've maintained our weight for fifteen years.

Any change in diet should be discussed with your doctor. I am a chef and the only thing I can diagnose is why your butter sauce broke! I urge you to check with your doctor before proceeding. Just don't ask your doctor for any recipes—I'll leave the health advice to your doctor, but the cooking is *my* job!

Low-Carb Substitutions

As an advocate of eating fresh foods, all of the ingredients used in the recipes in this book should be available at any grocery store. Though I love to reinvent things and "experiment" in the kitchen, I make it a point to keep my food "real" and as natural as I can. Real food is not just better for you, it tastes better as well!

That said, I would like to give a little information on the only three ingredients used in this book that I would consider "uncommon." These "uncommon" ingredients are sugar substitutes, almond flour, and milled flax seed—all three of which are now available in nearly every grocery store.

Sugar Substitutes – It's YOUR Choice!

Over my years on a low-carb lifestyle, nothing has been as hotly debated as sugar substitutes. People can be very opinionated about them and rightly so, as we should all question and research exactly what goes into our food, and then into our bodies. Sugar substitutes often bring into question what is and isn't natural, and for those eating only natural foods (as we try to do on low-carb), that is quite understandable.

As a chef, I voted with my palate first and foremost. Over a decade ago, I chose to use Splenda® (sucralose) as my sugar substitute of choice, and have stuck with it ever since. That said, that is simply my preference, and the sugar substitute you choose is entirely up to YOU.

Today, there are an incredible number of new sugar substitutes on the market, many of them entirely natural in every way. This is a luxury that simply did not exist when my family lost our weight over a decade ago. Back then, Splenda was brand new, and your only other alternatives came in blue or pink packets. Now you have erythritol, stevia, monk fruit, and agave, amongst others. These

and others are sold under many brand names including EZ-Sweetz, Nevella, Swerve, Steviva Blend, Truvia, Just Like Sugar, and Organic Zero. The only type of sugar substitute I would recommend against is xylitol, as I understand it can cause digestive discomfort and is poisonous to dogs.

The recipes in this book that call for sugar substitute are all measured equal to sugar to make them easy to follow, no matter which substitute is your preference. If you are using a brand of sugar substitute that does not measure the same as sugar, simply follow the directions on the package to measure out the correct amount for your brand.

Liquid versions of the sweeteners listed above tend to have the least carbohydrates, as they do not need any type of fillers to bulk them up. However, these usually measure the least like sugar, so be sure to follow their directions for measuring!

It's important to remember that sugar substitutes are actually some of the most studied foods on the planet (nobody is doing studies on celery). When in doubt, read the studies and the conclusions of those who made them, then make your own conclusions. I made my choice long ago and feel comfortable knowing that I've eliminated sugar and corn syrup from my life. As controversial as sugar substitutes may be, it's generally well accepted that eating excess sugar can raise your risk for diabetes and other diseases, especially if you are overweight.

Regardless of which sugar substitute is your preference, please be sure it is "heat stable" before baking with it. For instance, aspartame (which I do NOT recommend) is not heat stable and loses its sweetness when baked.

Finally, I would like to make one last recommendation that I have not made in the past. If you purchased this book to eat less or no gluten, not to watch your weight, it is perfectly acceptable and your choice to use actual sugar in my recipes. Over the years, I've noticed that many of my fans buy my books due to gluten allergies/sensitivities, and that these people don't have an issue with their weight. In these cases, if you are not at risk for diabetes and feel comfortable eating sugar, by all means do it!

Baking with Almond Flour

The only "flour" used in this book is Almond Flour (page 14) that we make ourselves from nothing but raw almonds. You can also purchase almond flour or "almond meal" in most grocery stores, usually sold in the organic, baking, or gluten-free departments. Store-bought almond flour is usually more expensive than making it yourself, and can also be a little more dry once baked, but it can be convenient to know it can be purchased in a pinch.

While almonds do contain fat, this fat is the good (monounsaturated) kind and is not something that should be frowned upon. At first glance, many of our baked goods will look high in fat due to our use of almond flour, but the numbers are not as important as where the fat comes from. In fact, many people believe adding almonds to your diet is better for maintaining a healthy weight.

Baking with Milled Flax Seed

Milled flax seed is made from natural seeds that have been ground into a coarse flour-like consistency. Also known as "flax seed meal," you can usually find it in the organic or gluten-free baking sections of the grocery store. The most popular brands available in stores are Hodgson Mill and Bob's Red Mill.

When used in baking, milled flax seed gives low-carb baked goods a heartier, more wheat-like flavor. It also adds a good amount of omega-3 fatty acids and fiber, both very good things!

Nutritional Information

The nutritional analysis provided in these recipes is meant only as a reference. It was compiled to the best of our ability using nutritional analysis software with an extremely large database of ingredients. Due to differences in the sizes of vegetables, brands of certain foods, or fat content of meat, your calculations may vary.

Calculations are for each serving of the finished dish. Calories in this book were rounded to the nearest 5, and all other amounts were rounded to the nearest .5 of a gram. Optional garnishes or variations were not included in the calculations. Recipes that include the use of another recipe (such as frosting for a cake) already include the nutritional information for the additional recipe as part of the overall dish.

Though we provide the nutritional information, our family has always made it a point to not count each and every gram of carbohydrates or calories. It is our belief that if you stock your house full of great natural foods and do not "cheat," you'll be eating well. I've found that, for many people, counting carbs can lead you to eat worse by trying to save up or "bank" your carbs to eat something you probably shouldn't be eating. Starving yourself all day to eat a whole pint of ice cream at night has never and will never be a good choice!

George, Rachel, Christian, Elise, and Anthony

Your Low-Carb Pantry

The following is a list of the most commonly used ingredients in this book and in our household. We try to keep most of these ingredients on hand at all times—that way we are ready to prepare nearly anything!

Spice Cabinet

- Baking powder
- Basil
- Bay leaves
- Black pepper
- Cayenne pepper
- Chili powder
- Cinnamon
- Coconut extract
- Cumin
- Garlic powder
- Italian seasoning
- Kosher salt
- Nutmeg
- Olive oil
- Onion powder
- Oregano
- Paprika
- Pumpkin pie spice
- Thyme
- Vanilla extract
- Vegetable oil
- White pepper

Pantry

- Almond flour or raw almonds
- Canned pumpkin
- Dijon mustard
- Garlic bulbs
- Milled flax seed
- Nonstick cooking spray
- Pecans
- Red onions
- Roasted red peppers
- Spaghetti squash
- Sugar substitute
- Unsweetened baking chocolate
- Unsweetened cocoa powder
- Worcestershire sauce

Fridge

- Almond milk (unsweetened)
- Bell peppers
- Butter
- Cilantro
- Cream Cheese
- Eggs
- Fresh herbs
- Half-and-half
- Heavy cream
- Lemons
- Limes
- Parmesan cheese
- Parsley
- Ricotta cheese

Shop the outer aisles of the grocery store . . . that's where all the naturally low-carb fresh food is located!

STAPLES

PREP TIME	COOK TIME	SERVES
10 min	0 min	10+

ALMOND FLOUR
The Secret to Low-Carb Baked Goods

Almond Flour has been used in baking by French chefs long before we had super-processed and bleached white flour. It's simple to see why pastry chefs always keep Almond Flour on hand—it tastes great and stays moist in baked goods. Even though almonds contain fat that regular flour does not, it's important to remember that this fat is monounsaturated "good fat," and that studies have shown that eating a serving of almonds a day actually boosts weight loss, regardless of the calories or fat.

SHOPPING LIST

10 ounces sliced raw almonds (may use whole raw almonds)

Calories: 140
Fat: 12g
Protein: 5g
Fiber: 3g
Net Carbs: 2g

1 GRIND the almonds on high in a food processor for about 3 minutes, until they've reached a grainy, flour-like consistency.

2 ALMOND Flour can be stored in an airtight container for up to 1 week on the counter or for several months in the freezer.

HELPFUL TIPS

For the smoothest and most flour-like consistency, start the almonds by grinding them in a food processor, and then run them (in small batches) through a coffee grinder. This is best for recipes where a smoother texture is expected, as with cookies.

Use slivered almonds to make "blanched" Almond Flour that is a lighter color.

LOW-CARB PIZZA CRUST
Makes Two 10-inch Pizza Crusts

Milled flax seed by itself is pure fiber, and therefore contains zero carbs! When mixed with other low-carb baking ingredients like almond flour and Parmesan cheese, it makes for a perfect pizza crust that looks whole wheat—without any wheat at all!

SHOPPING LIST

1 cup milled flax seed

½ cup Almond Flour (page 14)

½ cup grated Parmesan cheese

3 large eggs

½ teaspoon baking powder

1 teaspoon dry oregano

¼ teaspoon garlic powder

⅛ teaspoon onion powder

¼ teaspoon salt

Calories: 150
Fat: 12g
Protein: 9.5g
Fiber: 4.5g
Net Carbs: 1g

Make sure you pre-bake the crust before topping it and baking again!

1 PREHEAT oven to 350°, and line two 9 or 10-inch pizza pans with parchment paper.

2 ADD all ingredients to a bowl, and mix well to create a sticky dough.

3 CUT the dough in half, and place equal amounts of the dough on each of the prepared pizza pans. Cover dough with plastic wrap and use a heavy can or rolling pin over the top of the plastic to spread the dough out evenly, getting it as close to the edges of the pan as you can. Remove the plastic wrap.

4 BAKE the pizza crusts for 10–12 minutes, just until they start to brown. Use to create your favorite pizzas. Can be stored in the refrigerator or freezer until ready for use.

5 BAKE your favorite pizzas on the pre-baked crust at 350°, just until toppings are hot and/or melted.

HELPFUL TIPS

You can also use this dough to make one large rectangle pizza on a sheet pan lined with parchment paper.

BARBECUE SAUCE
No Sugar Added and Made From Scratch

Store-bought barbecue sauce is usually loaded with more corn syrup than almost any other ingredient, so it was one of the first things we had to reinvent when we started a low-carb lifestyle. Today, we always keep a jar of our own homemade sauce in the fridge for quick and easy barbecue dinners.

SHOPPING LIST

1 (15-ounce) can tomato sauce

3 ounces tomato paste

1 tablespoon white vinegar

1 tablespoon liquid smoke

2 teaspoons Worcestershire sauce

½ teaspoon hot sauce

½ cup sugar substitute

1 teaspoon minced garlic

¾ teaspoon onion powder

⅛ teaspoon garlic powder

1 teaspoon salt

½ teaspoon black pepper

Calories: 20
Fat: 0g
Protein: 1g
Fiber: 0.5g
Net Carbs: 3g

1 IN a mixing bowl, combine all ingredients, stirring until smooth. Leftovers should be refrigerated or frozen. Keeps for up to two weeks.

HELPFUL TIPS

When shopping for canned tomato sauce, be sure to buy "tomato sauce" and not a prepared pasta sauce. You should also read the ingredients to find a brand that doesn't add any additional sugar or corn syrup.

Try adding a drop of maple extract for even more flavor!

COMPOUND BUTTERS

Scampi, Dill, Ginger, and Gorgonzola Compound Butters

Compound butter is a chef's best friend. Because butter absorbs flavors with ease, adding ingredients directly into the butter makes for tons of flavor when using in recipes, or simply topping finished chicken or steak.

SHOPPING LIST

MASTER RECIPE

½ cup (1 stick) unsalted butter, softened

Juice of 1 lemon

2 teaspoons minced fresh garlic

2 tablespoons minced red onion

½ teaspoon garlic powder

1½ teaspoons salt

¼ teaspoon black pepper

1 pinch white pepper

Calories: 70
Fat: 7.5g
Protein: 0g
Fiber: 0g
Net Carbs: 0g

1 IN a bowl, whisk together all Master Recipe ingredients and additional ingredients for your chosen butter that are listed below. It takes a bit of work at first, but if you keep whisking, it will combine smoothly.

2 SPOON the Compound Butter onto a piece of plastic wrap and form it into a log about 2 inches around. Roll the plastic wrap up into a cylinder and twist the ends shut. Refrigerate at least 1 hour before slicing to cook with or top a dish.

SCAMPI BUTTER: Add an additional 1 teaspoon minced garlic, 1 tablespoon of chopped fresh parsley, and a dash of Worcestershire sauce.

DILL BUTTER: Add 1 tablespoon of chopped fresh dill and a dash of Worcestershire sauce.

GINGER BUTTER: Add 2 teaspoons minced ginger and a dash of low-sodium soy sauce.

GORGONZOLA BUTTER: Add 3 tablespoons Gorgonzola and 1 tablespoon chopped fresh chives.

Try making your own Compound Butters by adding ingredients to my master recipe.

BLACKENING SPICE
Our Must-Have Cajun Seasoning Blend

Store-bought seasoning blends almost always include either sugar or some form of the dreaded MSG (which can be labeled as so many different things these days). Thankfully, I've been making my own blackening spice mixture for decades and can say that it is not only better without fillers, but cheaper, as you most likely already have the ingredients in your spice rack.

SHOPPING LIST

5 tablespoons kosher salt

5 tablespoons paprika

1 tablespoon dried thyme

1 tablespoon black pepper

1 tablespoon garlic powder

½ teaspoon cayenne pepper

½ teaspoon ground white pepper

Calories: 5
Fat: 0g
Protein: 0g
Fiber: 0g
Net Carbs: 0g

1 Mix all ingredients together.

2 Store in an airtight container or empty spice canister.

HELPFUL TIPS

If you do not have any kosher salt on hand, you can simply substitute 2½ tablespoons of regular salt. The rule of thumb is that kosher salt is double the measure of regular salt.

This master seasoning goes great on chicken, beef, pork, and especially seafood. It's about as versatile as a spice mix gets!

PREP TIME	COOK TIME	SERVES
10 min	0 min	10

ITALIAN HERB RUB
A Great Use for Extra Fresh Herbs

Our garden is always brimming with more fresh herbs than we could ever use, but even people without a garden often let fresh herbs wilt in their refrigerator. This rub is not only an easy way to cook with fresh herbs, but can extend the lifespan of your herbs by three weeks!

SHOPPING LIST

½ cup fresh oregano leaves, stemmed and washed

½ cup fresh basil, stemmed and washed

½ cup fresh flat-leaf parsley, stemmed and washed

¼ cup extra virgin olive oil

¼ cup vegetable oil

2 tablespoons kosher salt

1½ teaspoons black pepper

2 teaspoons garlic powder

2 teaspoons onion powder

Calories: 110
Fat: 11g
Protein: 0g
Fiber: 0g
Net Carbs: 0g

1 PLACE all ingredients in a food processor and blend on high for about 1 minute, until well combined.

2 REMOVE and refrigerate for as long as 3 weeks in a plastic or glass container (metal containers may turn the herbs brown).

HELPFUL TIPS

If you'd like to cut back on the oil, try using half the amount, which will make for a thicker rub, easily thinned by a bit of water just before use.

This simple recipe can be used to make a rub out of any combination of fresh herbs.

CHOCOLATE GANACHE
DECADENT AND DARK DIPPING CHOCOLATE

At some point, we realized that nearly all of our chocolate dessert recipes started with this exact same method for making Chocolate Ganache. It was then that we thought, if you are a "chocoholic," this is a technique you should definitely master, leaving you to easily start making chocolate desserts as quickly as we do.

SHOPPING LIST

1 tablespoon butter

½ cup sugar substitute

2 teaspoons half-and-half

1 ounce unsweetened baking chocolate, chopped

1 teaspoon vanilla extract

Calories: 40
Fat: 3.5g
Protein: 0.5g
Fiber: 0.5g
Net Carbs: 2g

This Chocolate Ganache is a must for nearly all of our chocolate desserts!

1 FILL a pot with 2 inches of water, and place over medium-high heat, bringing the water up to a simmer. Place a stainless steel or tempered glass bowl over the pot to create a double boiler.

2 ADD the butter, sugar substitute, and half-and-half to the bowl of the double boiler, and mix with a spatula until combined.

3 ADD the chopped chocolate and stir, just until chocolate has melted and all is combined.

4 REMOVE from the heat and stir in vanilla extract. Use immediately, while still warm.

HELPFUL TIPS

Be careful not to overcook the chocolate, or it may get too thick or even break. Once it has just melted, quickly remove from the heat.

ALMOND FLOUR PIE CRUST
YOUR START TO LOW—CARB PIE BAKING

With this pie crust made from almond flour, you can start reinventing your favorite pies for a low-carb lifestyle. For the absolute best looking pies, make almond flour from blanched or slivered almonds (without the almond skin) for that clean, golden appearance.

SHOPPING LIST

2 cups Almond Flour (page 14), made from blanched almonds

¼ cup sugar substitute

2 tablespoons butter, softened

1 large egg

Dash of salt

Calories: 170
Fat: 15g
Protein: 6g
Fiber: 3g
Net Carbs: 2g

1 ADD all ingredients to a food processor and pulse until a dough is formed.

2 PREHEAT oven to 350°.

3 TAKE the dough and press it down evenly over the bottom of an 8 or 9-inch pie pan. Bake for 10–12 minutes, until lightly browned. Let cool before filling.

HELPFUL HINTS

I don't recommend baking this crust in disposable pie pans, as they heat less evenly and can warp, cracking the crust.

This crust can be frozen for even easier pies any time!

WHIPPED CREAM
You Can't Top This Perfect Topping

Whipping cream is a kitchen technique everyone should know, but cans and tubs of processed "stuff" is still flying off the shelves. Some "whipped toppings" are nothing more than whipped corn syrup and trans-fat (even "sugar-free" versions can contain corn syrup), so it should go without saying that nothing beats the real thing! Making it yourself also allows you to choose your sugar substitute of choice.

SHOPPING LIST

1 cup heavy cream

⅓ cup sugar substitute

1 teaspoon vanilla extract

Calories: 35
Fat: 3.5g
Protein: 0.5g
Fiber: 0g
Net Carbs: 1g

1 IN an electric mixer on high speed, whip the heavy cream until frothy.

2 ADD the sugar substitute and vanilla extract, and whip on high speed until soft peaks form. Serve immediately.

HELPFUL TIPS

Properly whipped cream should be fluffy, not stiff. If the cream starts to look lumpy or begins to bunch together, you are overwhipping it.

Leftover whipped cream should be stored in a covered glass dish, but will deflate over time.

BUTTERCREAM CHEESE FROSTING
Or Any Flavor Low-Carb Frosting

This "master" low-carb frosting recipe uses real butter and cream cheese to combine the best of both your typical buttercream and cream cheese frostings. The vanilla extract can be swapped for any type of extract to match the baked goods you are frosting.

SHOPPING LIST

6 tablespoons butter, softened

16 ounces cream cheese, softened

1 cup sugar substitute

1 tablespoon vanilla extract

Calories: 180
Fat: 18.5g
Protein: 3g
Fiber: 0g
Net Carbs: 1g

1　BEAT all ingredients in an electric mixer on high until light and fluffy.

2　SPREAD on a completely cooled cake or baked goods.

HELPFUL TIPS

You should definitely substitute coconut extract in place of the vanilla extract when making this frosting to frost my Coconut Cake (page 207).

Warning: You must resist the urge to eat frosting straight out of the bowl.

Denver Breakfast Pizza

Mixed Berry Muffins

Eggs Florentine Skillet

BREAKFAST

EGGS FLORENTINE SKILLET

A Breakfast Spinach Sauté, Topped with a Whole Egg

This skillet with spinach, pancetta, and onion makes a full breakfast for two. Whole eggs are cooked right over the top of the spinach in the pan, and then sprinkled with Parmesan cheese before serving. If your pan is large enough, you can easily split this into four servings by cracking two additional eggs into the pan.

SHOPPING LIST

1 tablespoon olive oil

¼ cup diced pancetta (see tip)

5 ounces fresh spinach

¼ cup diced red onion

1 teaspoon minced garlic

2 large eggs

Salt and pepper

2 tablespoons shredded Parmesan cheese (may use grated)

Diced tomato, for garnish

Calories: 250
Fat: 20g
Protein: 14g
Fiber: 2g
Net Carbs: 2.5g

1 HEAT the olive oil in a skillet over medium heat. Add the pancetta to the pan, and cook until it begins to crisp.

2 ADD the spinach, red onion, and garlic, and sauté until the spinach cooks down, about 3 minutes.

3 CRACK the eggs over the spinach and lightly season all with salt and pepper. Cover and let cook until the steam has cooked the whites of the eggs.

4 UNCOVER, sprinkle Parmesan cheese over all, and garnish with diced tomato. Serve immediately.

HELPFUL TIPS

Some stores sell Boar's Head brand diced pancetta in the gourmet deli section. Otherwise, you can usually ask the deli counter for a slice about ¼ inch thick to dice yourself.

Can't find pancetta? Simply substitute bacon, Canadian bacon, or diced ham.

MIXED BERRY MUFFINS
WITH FRESH BLUEBERRIES AND RASPBERRIES

We've been making delicious muffins using Almond Flour (page 14) for nearly a decade now. Lately, we've had a lot of extra berries from our garden and we love to bake them into these muffins. Blueberries and raspberries will give you the best results, but small blackberries are also recommended!

SHOPPING LIST

Nonstick cooking spray

4 large eggs

2 cups Almond Flour (page 14)

¾ cup sugar substitute

2 teaspoons vanilla extract

2 teaspoons baking powder

⅛ teaspoon salt

¼ cup blueberries

⅓ cup raspberries

Calories: 120
Fat: 9.5g
Protein: 5.5g
Fiber: 2.5g
Net Carbs: 3g

1 PLACE oven rack in the center position, and preheat to 375°. Grease a 12-cup muffin pan with nonstick cooking spray.

2 IN a large bowl, beat eggs until frothy. Add the Almond Flour, sugar substitute, vanilla extract, baking powder, and salt, and mix well, creating a batter.

3 GENTLY fold the berries into the batter and fill each of the greased muffin cups ⅔ of the way full.

4 BAKE 20–25 minutes, until the tops of the muffins turn a light golden brown and a toothpick stuck into the center of one comes out mostly clean. Let cool 10 minutes before serving.

HELPFUL TIPS

Any combination of fresh berries can be used; however, very ripe strawberries are not recommended, as they let out a lot of water as the muffins bake.

Baking in a silicone muffin pan will ensure that your muffins release cleanly.

BETTER CHEDDAR SAUSAGE & EGG CUPS

Your Breakfast, Baked in Muffin Cups

This technique has become my favorite way to make breakfast for a crowd, and I'm surprised I didn't use it at home earlier. Baking eggs in muffin tins like I do in this recipe is actually an old chef's trick I used to use for making perfect "poached" eggs in large numbers.

SHOPPING LIST

Nonstick cooking spray

6 ounces breakfast sausage, cooked and crumbled

6 large eggs

1 cup shredded Cheddar cheese

Calories: 240
Fat: 18g
Protein: 16.5g
Fiber: 0g
Net Carbs: 0.5g

Serve topped with a dollop of sour cream and chopped chives as garnish!

1 PLACE oven rack in the center position, and preheat oven to 375°.

2 SPRAY a 6-cup muffin tin with nonstick cooking spray and divide the cooked crumbled sausage equally into each of the 6 cups.

3 CRACK an egg into each of the 6 cups over top of the sausage, trying to keep the yolks unbroken.

4 BAKE for 12–14 minutes, or until the egg whites are no longer runny.

5 REMOVE from oven and top each cooked egg with equal amounts of Cheddar cheese. Bake an additional 1–2 minutes, just until the cheese has melted.

6 LET the eggs cool in the muffin tin for 2 minutes to set before removing with a fork to serve. (They should hold together like a muffin.)

HELPFUL TIPS

We love these made with leftover cooked Italian sausage and marinara sauce, topped with mozzarella cheese! Or even pepperoni!

MAPLE SILVER DOLLAR PANCAKES

Wheatless and Worth Their Weight in Silver

Let's face it, ordinary pancakes are nothing but stacks of starch that need to be fried in tons of oil and topped with syrup to have any flavor. My recipe uses healthy almonds and flax in place of high-carb flour, and adds maple extract so that you don't even need to top them with sugary syrup.

SHOPPING LIST

Nonstick cooking spray

2 large eggs

¼ cup water

1 tablespoon maple extract

½ cup Almond Flour (page 14)

¼ cup milled flax seed

¼ cup sugar substitute

½ teaspoon baking powder

½ teaspoon baking soda

⅛ teaspoon salt

Calories: 145
Fat: 11g
Protein: 7g
Fiber: 3.5g
Net Carbs: 2g

1 SPRAY a griddle or large nonstick skillet with nonstick cooking spray, and heat over medium heat.

2 STIR together all ingredients with a wooden spoon, until a well-blended batter is formed.

3 POUR approximately 16 silver-dollar-sized cakes onto the hot griddle, and cook on the first side for 3–4 minutes, or until they are golden brown on the bottom.

4 FLIP and cook for just 1 additional minute. Serve immediately.

HELPFUL TIPS

Serve these topped with butter or whipped cream. For something more syrupy, try using natural agave nectar!

I can fit all 16 pancakes on a large griddle, but if you are using a pan, you will need to cook in smaller batches.

CINNAMON BUN MINUTE MUFFIN

Sweet Cinnamon Goodness, Made in a Minute

One-minute muffins or OMMs as they are referred to in the low-carb world, can be made in all ways, from savory to sweet! This sweet recipe was invented to duplicate the memories I have of the decadent (and dangerous) cinnamon buns that you can always smell as you walk through a mall.

SHOPPING LIST

¼ cup Almond Flour (page 14)

1 tablespoon milled flax seed (golden is best)

1 large egg

2 tablespoons sugar substitute

½ teaspoon baking powder

1 teaspoon melted butter

½ teaspoon ground cinnamon

Calories: 340
Fat: 27g
Protein: 19g
Fiber: 5g
Net Carbs: 4g

1 ADD all ingredients to a microwave-safe coffee mug, and mix with a fork until well combined.

2 MICROWAVE for about 1 minute on HIGH, or until batter rises in cup, and a toothpick stuck into the center comes out mostly clean. Microwaves vary, but 1 minute seems to be the minimum cooking time, so start there and add a few seconds, if needed.

3 LET cool 3 minutes before serving.

HELPFUL TIPS

These are much better when topped with my Buttercream Cheese Frosting (page 23).

I like to add a few pecans into the batter as well.

SCOTCH EGGS

Eggs with Sausage and a Crispy Breading

This recipe comes to me from "across the pond," where it is a classic right up there with shepherd's pie. Scotch Eggs are basically hard-boiled eggs wrapped in sausage and breaded with a crisp breading. It's the kind of thing low-carb allows you to enjoy without the guilt you'd have on a low-fat diet.

SHOPPING LIST

4 cups trans-fat-free frying oil

2 large eggs

¼ cup water

¼ cup Almond Flour (page 14)

¼ cup grated Parmesan cheese

¼ teaspoon salt

⅛ teaspoon black pepper

⅛ teaspoon garlic powder

1 pound ground raw
   breakfast sausage

6 hard-boiled eggs, peeled

Calories: 305
Fat: 20g
Protein: 29g
Fiber: 0.5g
Net Carbs: 1g

These are best served with hot sauce to drizzle over top.

1 ADD the frying oil to a heavy pot, leaving at least 4 inches to the top, and place over medium-high heat, or use an electric deep fryer filled to the fill line and preheated to 350°.

2 IN a medium bowl, whisk the eggs and water to make an egg wash.

3 IN a larger bowl, mix the Almond Flour, Parmesan, salt, pepper, and garlic powder.

4 DIVIDE the ground sausage into 6 even amounts, and, using your hands, work the sausage around each of the hard-boiled eggs to seal the egg in a sausage coating.

5 DIP each sausage-wrapped egg first into the egg wash and then into the breading, making sure to coat well.

6 PAT off any excess breading and carefully place each breaded egg, one at a time, into the hot oil. Fry until golden brown and crisp, about 2 minutes. Transfer to paper towels to drain.

HELPFUL TIPS

You can easily bake these by placing the breaded eggs on a parchment paper-lined sheet pan and baking at 375° for 30 minutes. If they need further crisping, just finish under the broiler for 1 minute.

PREP TIME	COOK TIME	SERVES
15 min	20 min	4

SOUTHWESTERN FRITTATA
A One-Pan Breakfast Casserole

Frittatas are like foolproof omelets that are so easy to make that they should be a staple of every person's morning. This Southwestern Frittata includes some of my favorite fresh ingredients, but the basic method used here can be adapted to make any frittata you can dream of.

SHOPPING LIST

1 tablespoon olive oil

¼ cup diced red bell pepper

¼ cup diced red onion

2 teaspoons diced jalapeño

1 teaspoon minced garlic

6 large eggs

¼ cup half-and-half

¼ teaspoon salt

⅛ teaspoon black pepper

1 tablespoon chopped cilantro

¼ cup shredded Cheddar-Jack cheese

Diced avocado, for garnish

Calories: 195
Fat: 15g
Protein: 12g
Fiber: 0g
Net Carbs: 2.5g

Try adding chorizo sausage for a spicy kick of protein!

1 PREHEAT oven to 325°.

2 HEAT the olive oil in an oven-proof skillet over medium heat. Add the bell pepper, red onion, jalapeño, and garlic, and sauté until peppers begin to sweat.

3 WHISK together the eggs, half-and-half, salt, black pepper, and cilantro, and pour over the vegetables in the skillet.

4 USING a rubber spatula, gently push the cooked egg from one side of the pan to the other to allow all of the raw egg to reach the bottom of the pan, and to prevent the bottom from burning. Continue this until the top of the eggs are only slightly runny.

5 SPRINKLE the cheese over top and bake 10–12 minutes, or until frittata puffs up, and cheese begins to brown. Let cool 3 minutes before serving garnished with diced avocado.

HELPFUL TIPS

The diced avocado is only a suggestion, as you can garnish this in the same way you would garnish most southwestern dishes. Salsa, guacamole, sour cream—the decision is yours!

DENVER BREAKFAST PIZZA

Denver Gave Us an Omelet and I Made a Pizza

An omelet on a pizza and it's still low-carb? You bet! This Denver Breakfast Pizza has all the flavors you love about the omelet on my Low-Carb Pizza Crust. I've found that placing the cheese under the scrambled eggs makes this hold together better, but you may still want to grab a fork for this one.

SHOPPING LIST

1 Low-Carb Pizza Crust (page 15)

¾ cup grated Cheddar cheese

1 tablespoon butter

6 large eggs, beaten

¼ teaspoon salt

⅛ teaspoon pepper

¼ cup chopped Canadian bacon

2 tablespoons sliced scallions

2 tablespoons diced green
   bell pepper

2 tablespoons diced red bell pepper

Calories: 380
Fat: 28g
Protein: 26g
Fiber: 4.5g
Net Carbs: 3g

1 PREHEAT oven to 350°.

2 TOP the pre-baked pizza crust with the Cheddar cheese.

3 HEAT the butter in a skillet over medium heat. Add the eggs and scramble with the salt and pepper. Scramble just until they can hold together, but are still somewhat runny.

4 DISTRIBUTE the scrambled eggs over the cheese on the pizza crust and top with the Canadian bacon, scallions, and bell peppers.

5 BAKE 7–8 minutes, just until cheese has melted and vegetables begin to sweat. Let cool 3 minutes before slicing to serve.

HELPFUL TIPS

For a better presentation, thinly slice the vegetables in strips, and leave the Canadian bacon whole. (However, truthfully, this is harder to eat.)

Reserve a small amount of the Cheddar cheese to lightly sprinkle over the top of the eggs to add a pop of orange color.

EGGPLANT AND BACON HOME FRIES

Eggplant for Breakfast? You Bet!

We usually have more eggplant growing in our garden than we know what to do with. A simple sauté like this one has now become a staple of our morning breakfasts—it's the perfect low-carb alternative to starchy home fries!

SHOPPING LIST

1 teaspoon paprika

½ teaspoon kosher salt

¼ teaspoon black pepper

¼ teaspoon garlic powder

4 pieces cooked bacon, chopped

2 tablespoons chopped
    yellow onion

2 tablespoons chopped green
    bell pepper

1½ cups cubed eggplant with skin
    (about 1 medium-size eggplant)

2 tablespoons olive oil

Calories: 210
Fat: 16g
Protein: 10.5g
Fiber: 1.5g
Net Carbs: 1g

1 PLACE all of the ingredients, except the eggplant and olive oil, in a large mixing bowl, and toss to combine.

2 ADD the cubed eggplant to the mixing bowl, and toss with a fork to thoroughly coat each piece.

3 HEAT the olive oil in a nonstick sauté pan over medium heat. Add the eggplant mixture to the pan, and cook for 2–3 minutes before gently stirring.

4 LET cook an additional 2–3 minutes, or until the eggplant pieces are well browned. Serve hot as a breakfast or dinner side dish!

HELPFUL TIPS

We find that smaller eggplants, or Ichibon (Japanese) eggplants seem to work the best in this recipe, as they have fewer seeds and are more firm for frying. Two Ichibon eggplants are the perfect amount for this recipe.

Be careful not to stir the eggplant too much while cooking, or it may not brown, and may fall apart. Let the pan do the work!

CINNAMON WHEATLESS WAFFLES
NO WAFFLING AROUND ON THIS ONE

Waffle irons are extremely inexpensive now, and a great way to kick up your low-carb breakfast. Without any wheat or added sugar, these waffles are proof that a low-carb breakfast isn't just eggs and bacon.

SHOPPING LIST

Nonstick cooking spray

½ cup Almond Flour (page 14)

¼ cup sugar substitute

½ teaspoon baking powder

2 large eggs

⅓ cup unsweetened almond milk

⅓ cup water

1 tablespoon vegetable oil

1 teaspoon vanilla extract

½ teaspoon ground cinnamon

Calories: 180
Fat: 15g
Protein: 7.5g
Fiber: 2g
Net Carbs: 2.5g

I serve these hot out of the iron with butter, fresh fruit, and whipped cream.

1 SPRAY an electric waffle iron with nonstick cooking spray and let preheat.

2 IN a large bowl, combine all ingredients until a thick but smooth consistency is reached. If the batter is not smooth or is too thick, add a small amount of additional water.

3 POUR ¼ cup batter in the center of the waffle iron and close the lid. Cook for 5 minutes, or until steam is no longer coming out of the sides of the waffle iron.

4 REPEAT until all batter is used. The ¼ cup of batter per waffle is the perfect amount for a smaller waffle iron, and should make 6 waffles. Larger waffle irons will require ⅓ cup batter, ½ cup for a Belgian-sized waffle.

5 SERVE hot, with butter, for that "cinnamon toast" experience, and even top them with fresh fruit and sugar-free whipped cream, if desired!

HELPFUL TIPS

Do not open the waffle iron during the first 3 minutes. Some batter may escape out of the sides, but that is normal until you get used to the proper amount for your waffle iron.

COCONUT FLAPJACKS

Will Have You Doing Jumping Jacks (Maybe)

These delicious flapjacks are not only wheat-free, but free of any type of flour at all! Reading the recipe, you may think it is a mistake, but I assure you that these cook up great and, more importantly, they taste great as well!

SHOPPING LIST

4 ounces cream cheese, softened

4 large eggs

⅓ cup sugar substitute

½ teaspoon coconut extract

2 tablespoons coconut oil (may use vegetable oil)

¼ cup unsweetened coconut flakes, for garnish

Calories: 215
Fat: 20g
Protein: 8.5g
Fiber: 0g
Net Carbs: 1g

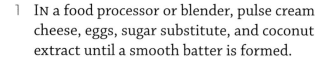

1 IN a food processor or blender, pulse cream cheese, eggs, sugar substitute, and coconut extract until a smooth batter is formed.

2 COAT the inside of an 8-inch nonstick pan with a teaspoon of coconut oil, and place over medium heat.

3 ONCE the pan is hot, add 2 tablespoons of the batter and tilt the pan side to side until the mix almost covers the bottom.

4 COOK for about 2 minutes before flipping to cook 1 additional minute.

5 REPEAT the process until all batter is used. Serve sprinkled with unsweetened coconut.

HELPFUL TIPS

Top these flapjacks with berries and sugar-free whipped cream, or drizzle with agave nectar or a small amount of honey in place of syrup.

The batter in this recipe should make 8 large flapjacks.

RICOTTA CRÊPES

Easy to Make, Easier to Eat

Crêpes are mostly egg as it is, so adapting this flourless version was a no-brainer. The filling options are limitless (see my tips below), but if you are thinking of making a savory filling, I'd suggest leaving the vanilla, cinnamon, and sugar substitute out of the batter. Makes 4 crêpes.

SHOPPING LIST

¼ cup whole milk ricotta cheese

2 large eggs

2 tablespoons sugar substitute

¼ teaspoon ground cinnamon

½ teaspoon vanilla extract

4 teaspoons butter, divided

Calories: 95
Fat: 7.5g
Protein: 5g
Fiber: 0g
Net Carbs: 1g

I like to fill these with whipped cream, and top with sautéed berries.

1 WHISK together ricotta, eggs, sugar substitute, cinnamon, and vanilla extract, until well combined.

2 HEAT 1 teaspoon of the butter in an 8-inch nonstick skillet over medium heat.

3 DROP 2 heaping tablespoons of the crêpe batter into the hot pan, and immediately tilt the pan back and forth to make a thin coat across the bottom of the pan.

4 COOK only until the crêpe has set, about 1 minute, before carefully flipping to cook only 1 additional minute.

5 REPEAT steps 2–4 to make 3 additional crêpes.

HELPFUL TIPS

You can fill these with my Whipped Cream (page 22), and fresh berries or make a cannoli-style filling by combining ¼ cup ricotta cheese, 2 tablespoons sugar substitute, and ¼ teaspoon almond extract.

PREP TIME
5 min

COOK TIME
15 min

SERVES
6

MAPLE PECAN DROP SCONES

Freeform Breakfast "Bread"

These Maple Pecan Drop Scones make the perfect breakfast, especially when accompanied by a nice hot cup of coffee! You've got to start the day off right, and I can't think of a better way than with one (or two) of these.

SHOPPING LIST

2 large eggs, beaten until frothy

1 cup Almond Flour (page 14)

⅓ cup sugar substitute

1½ teaspoons baking powder

2 teaspoons maple extract

½ cup coarsely chopped pecans

Calories: 180
Fat: 16g
Protein: 6.5g
Fiber: 3g
Net Carbs: 2.5g

1 PREHEAT oven to 375°, and line a sheet pan with parchment paper.

2 IN a large bowl, combine the eggs, Almond Flour, sugar substitute, baking powder, and maple extract, mixing well to create a batter.

3 FOLD the pecans into the batter, and use a large spoon to drop 6 evenly spaced drops (about 2 heaping tablespoons each) of the batter onto the prepared pan.

4 BAKE for 15 minutes, or until scones begin to lightly brown. Let cool for 10 minutes before serving.

HELPFUL TIPS

If your batter is too thin to hold any form at all, simply add more Almond Flour until it is the consistency of a loose cookie dough.

Add a handful of fresh blueberries into the batter for Blueberry Pecan Scones.

Old-Fashioned Mock
Potato Salad with Egg

Grilled Eggplant Caprese Salad

California Beet Salad

LUNCH

CALIFORNIA BEET SALAD
WITH GOAT CHEESE AND TOASTED WALNUTS

Recently, we've added sweet potatoes into our low-carb way of life, and now my son, Christian, has convinced me that beets are just as good for you, if not better! So this recipe is for Christian, a California Beet Salad, just like the ones I used to make in my restaurant days.

SHOPPING LIST

3 beets (about ¾ pound)

¼ cup chopped walnuts

¼ cup red wine vinegar

½ teaspoon Dijon mustard

1 teaspoon sugar substitute

¼ teaspoon dried rosemary

¼ teaspoon salt

¼ cup walnut oil (may use olive oil)

3 cups arugula or fancy greens

4 thin slices red onion

2 ounces goat cheese, sliced

Calories: 205
Fat: 14.5g
Protein: 10g
Fiber: 3.5g
Net Carbs: 7g

Using walnut oil in the dressing is highly recommended. It takes this salad to a whole 'nother level!

1 PREHEAT oven to 425°. Remove greens from beets and scrub.

2 THOROUGHLY wrap the whole beats in aluminum foil and bake 1 hour.

3 MEANWHILE, place the walnuts in a dry skillet over medium heat and shake the pan until nuts are toasted and fragrant.

4 CREATE the vinaigrette by combining red wine vinegar, Dijon mustard, sugar substitute, rosemary, and salt. Whisk in walnut oil a little at a time until all is combined.

5 PEEL the roasted beets while still warm, then cool completely. Slice into thick slices.

6 ARRANGE a bed of arugula on 4 salad plates. Top with an equal amount of the sliced beets, toasted walnuts, red onion, and sliced goat cheese. Drizzle with the vinaigrette before serving.

HELPFUL TIPS

Canned or jarred beets can be used to make these salads, but only if they do not contain any added sugar, so be sure to read the ingredients! It should go without saying that the flavor of canned will be nowhere near as good.

CREAM OF ASPARAGUS SOUP

A DELICIOUSLY CREAMY SOUP, PACKED WITH FRESH ASPARAGUS

Thickening soups without adding carb-filled starches is not the easiest thing to do, which is why this recipe works so well—it's thickened by puréeing the asparagus into the broth and adding cream. Makes two large bowls.

SHOPPING LIST

1 tablespoon butter

8 ounces asparagus, ends trimmed

1 tablespoon minced red onion

1 teaspoon minced garlic

¼ teaspoon salt

¼ teaspoon black pepper

2½ cups chicken broth

½ cup heavy cream

Sour cream, for garnish

Calories: 270
Fat: 24g
Protein: 9g
Fiber: 2g
Net Carbs: 6g

For even more flavor, garnish with a dollop of fresh pesto in place of the sour cream.

1 HEAT the butter in a sauce pot over medium-high heat.

2 CUT the asparagus into 1-inch lengths and add to the pot, sautéing for 3 minutes.

3 ADD the red onion, garlic, salt, and pepper, and continue sautéing an additional 3 minutes.

4 POUR in the broth, raise the heat to high, and continue cooking until liquid has reduced by half, about 5 minutes.

5 REMOVE from the heat and (carefully!) purée using an immersion (hand) blender.

6 RETURN to the heat and stir in the heavy cream. Continue stirring, just until the soup is piping hot. Serve immediately, garnished with a dollop of sour cream.

HELPFUL TIPS

This same method can be used to make Cream of Broccoli Soup by substituting broccoli in place of the asparagus—you can even use frozen broccoli florets (though fresh will taste better).

TUNA SALAD STUFFED TOMATOES

TUNA CAUGHT IN A TOMATO NET

I'm always looking for more inventive way to present my dishes, especially using garnishes that are edible! That said, I wouldn't call the tomatoes in this recipe a garnish, as they are actually the bowls that hold the creamy tuna salad. Serve with a knife and fork, and dig right in!

SHOPPING LIST

4 medium tomatoes

Salt and pepper

1 can white (albacore)
  tuna, drained

¼ cup mayonnaise

2 stalks celery, finely diced

2 green onions, thinly sliced

1 teaspoon white wine vinegar

Calories: 160
Fat: 10.5g
Protein: 11g
Fiber: 2g
Net Carbs: 3.5g

1 SLICE the tops off tomatoes and use a spoon to hollow each out of seeds and membranes. Lightly season the inside of each with salt and pepper.

2 FOLD remaining ingredients together to create the tuna salad. Season to taste with salt and pepper.

3 SPOON an equal amount of the tuna salad into each tomato, and serve garnished with additional sliced green onions, if desired.

HELPFUL TIPS

Cider vinegar or lemon juice can be substituted for the white wine vinegar in a pinch.

Turn this into a party appetizer by stuffing cherry tomatoes in place of the regular tomatoes.

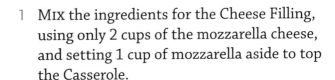

SCALLOPED SQUASH CASSEROLE WITH HAM
A POTLUCK CLASSIC THAT HAS ALWAYS BEEN LOW-CARB

Squash casseroles are a popular potluck dish that (depending on the recipe) is already low-carb! I'm a huge fan of this because it reminds me of scalloped potatoes— without all of the carbs, of course! By adding sliced ham, this can even be served as a full dinner.

SHOPPING LIST

CHEESE FILLING

15 ounces ricotta cheese

3 cups shredded mozzarella cheese, divided

2 large eggs

¼ teaspoon minced garlic

2 teaspoons Italian seasoning

½ teaspoon garlic powder

¼ teaspoon black pepper

CASSEROLE

Nonstick cooking spray

1½ pounds yellow squash, very thinly sliced

Salt and pepper

½ cup thinly sliced red onion

1 pound cooked sliced baked ham

Calories: 330
Fat: 19g
Protein: 29g
Fiber: 2g
Net Carbs: 6g

1 MIX the ingredients for the Cheese Filling, using only 2 cups of the mozzarella cheese, and setting 1 cup of mozzarella aside to top the Casserole.

2 PREHEAT oven to 350°, and spray a 13x9-inch baking dish with nonstick cooking spray.

3 LAYER the bottom of the baking dish with half of the yellow squash slices, and lightly season with salt and pepper. Top with half of the onion and half of the sliced ham. Top all with half of the Cheese Filling, spooning it on in dollops.

4 MAKE a second layer of squash, then onion, ham, and Cheese Filling. Top all with the reserved cup of mozzarella cheese.

5 BAKE for 50–60 minutes, or until the top is golden brown and bubbly. Let rest 5 minutes before serving.

HELPFUL TIPS

Leftover ham works great in this casserole, though sliced ham from the deli will work perfectly as well.

I (carefully!) use a mandolin slicer to cut the squash nice and thin.

ULTIMATE MOCK MAC AND CHEESE CASSEROLE
WITH BROCCOLI, CHICKEN, AND BACON

With cauliflower taking the place of macaroni, this satisfying casserole is chock-full of ingredients you may already have in the fridge. It's my famous Mock Mac and Cheese Casserole, only better (it has bacon)!

SHOPPING LIST

Nonstick cooking spray

1 large head cauliflower, chopped

1 cup chopped broccoli

1 cup cooked cubed chicken

¾ cup heavy cream

4 ounces cream cheese, sliced

1½ teaspoons Dijon mustard

½ teaspoon kosher salt

¼ teaspoon ground black pepper

⅛ teaspoon garlic powder

2 cups shredded Cheddar cheese, divided

6 ounces cooked bacon, chopped

Calories: 325
Fat: 25g
Protein: 20g
Fiber: 1.5g
Net Carbs: 3g

This is also a crowd-pleasing potluck dish!

1 PLACE the rack in the center position and preheat oven to 375°. Spray a 9x9-inch casserole dish with nonstick cooking spray. Bring a large pot of salted water to a boil.

2 COOK the cauliflower and broccoli in the boiling water for about 5 minutes, or until crisp yet tender. Drain well; pat between layers of paper towels to dry, and transfer to the prepared baking dish, along with the cooked chicken.

3 BRING the cream to a simmer in a small saucepan, and whisk in the cream cheese, mustard, salt, pepper, and garlic powder.

4 STIR in 1½ cups of the cheese and whisk for just a minute until melted and combined. Remove from the heat and pour over the ingredients in the casserole dish.

5 SPRINKLE the cooked bacon over all, top with the remaining ½ cup of Cheddar, and bake for 15 minutes, or until browned and bubbling. Let cool for 5 minutes before serving.

HELPFUL TIPS

Chunk baked ham may be used in place of the chicken, and try using Swiss or Gouda cheese in place of the Cheddar for a completely different casserole!

PREP TIME	CHILL TIME	SERVES
20 min	1 hour	8

OLD-FASHIONED MOCK POTATO SALAD WITH EGG

Our Famous Alternative to the Picnic Staple

This is one of my best reinventions of all time and is still one of the most popular low-carb recipes in the Food Network archives. The flavors are exactly what you'd expect from a traditional potato salad, but made with cauliflower—it's something you just have to try to understand!

SHOPPING LIST

1 large head cauliflower, cleaned

6 large eggs, hard-boiled, chopped

2 stalks celery, finely diced

1 cup mayonnaise

½ teaspoon yellow table mustard

½ teaspoon kosher salt

¼ teaspoon black pepper

⅛ teaspoon garlic powder

Paprika, for garnish

Fresh parsley, chopped, for garnish

Calories: 180
Fat: 13g
Protein: 6g
Fiber: 2g
Net Carbs: 3g

1 CHOP the cauliflower into small pieces (should make about 4 cups).

2 COOK the cauliflower pieces in boiling water for about 5 minutes, just until tender.

3 DRAIN cauliflower and immerse in an ice water bath to stop the cooking process.

4 DRAIN cauliflower well, and then pat dry between several layers of paper towels.

5 PLACE the cauliflower in a bowl with all of the remaining ingredients, except the garnishes, and fold together.

6 SPRINKLE with the paprika and parsley, and chill for at least 1 hour before serving.

HELPFUL TIPS

While it isn't as crisp, we've also successfully made this with frozen cauliflower florets that we've simply thawed and mixed into the salad without boiling.

Try garnishing with diced roasted red peppers for more color.

BROCCOLI & CHEDDAR SOUP
You'll Wonder Why They Even Sell Soup in a Can

I think I'm mostly correct in assuming that Broccoli & Cheddar Soup is just about everyone's favorite soup and one that I absolutely knew I had to reinvent for my low-carb lifestyle. Using an immersion (hand) blender makes it easy to blend some of the broccoli into the soup to thicken it, but you can also let it cool and transfer to an ordinary blender, then reheat.

SHOPPING LIST

4 tablespoons butter

¼ cup diced yellow onion

5 cups low-sodium chicken broth

1 head broccoli, chopped

1 bay leaf

½ teaspoon onion powder

¼ teaspoon black pepper

2 cups shredded sharp
  Cheddar cheese

1 cup heavy cream

Salt

Calories: 345
Fat: 28g
Protein: 16g
Fiber: 2g
Net Carbs: 4g

16 ounces of frozen broccoli can be used in place of fresh, if desired, though fresh is best!

1 HEAT the butter in a sauce pot over medium-high heat.

2 ADD the onion to the pot and sauté for 2 minutes.

3 POUR in chicken broth and add the chopped broccoli, bay leaf, onion powder, and pepper. Bring up to a simmer and then reduce heat to medium low. Cover and cook until broccoli is tender, about 20 minutes.

4 REMOVE from the heat and (carefully!) purée using an immersion (hand) blender, just until about ⅔ of the broccoli is smooth and the soup has thickened slightly.

5 RETURN to the heat and stir in heavy cream and shredded cheese. Raise heat to medium and simmer, stirring constantly, until cheese has melted and soup has slightly thickened further. Season with salt to taste before serving.

HELPFUL TIPS

For whatever reason, I've found that Kraft brand shredded sharp Cheddar cheese melts smoother than some other brands.

WALDORF COLESLAW

Creamy Slaw with Walnuts and Celery

This is one of our oldest and most popular recipes, not only with the fans, but in our own house. There is hardly a family get-together that Rachel doesn't whip up a batch of this Waldorf Coleslaw for the table—it beats a green salad any day!

SHOPPING LIST

½ cup sour cream

⅓ cup mayonnaise

⅓ cup sugar substitute

½ cup chopped walnuts

2 tablespoons red wine vinegar

16 ounces shredded cabbage

3 stalks celery, thinly sliced

¾ teaspoon salt

⅛ teaspoon black pepper

¼ teaspoon ground nutmeg

Calories: 105
Fat: 8.5g
Protein: 2.5g
Fiber: 2g
Net Carbs: 4g

1 COMBINE all ingredients in a large mixing bowl, tossing until fully mixed.

2 CAN serve immediately, but the flavor is best if you chill for at least 2 hours before serving.

HELPFUL TIPS

We use a combination of green and red cabbage to make this recipe, but just for aesthetic purposes. You can also use a bagged coleslaw mix, but the carrots included in it contain more carbs than cabbage on its own.

Adding ¼ cup of diced apple makes this even better while only adding 0.5 grams of carbs per serving!

GRILLED EGGPLANT CAPRESE SALAD
A Classic Salad Made Even Better

Caprese Salad is one of the easiest (and best) Italian dishes you can make, but if you really want to impress someone (or your tastebuds), you've got to try my take on it! The grilled eggplant literally adds a whole other layer to your classic Caprese.

SHOPPING LIST

1 medium eggplant

2 tablespoons olive oil

Salt and pepper

2 tomatoes

8 slices fresh mozzarella cheese

8 large leaves basil

2 tablespoons balsamic vinegar

1 tablespoon extra virgin olive oil

Calories: 285
Fat: 21g
Protein: 16g
Fiber: 4.5g
Net Carbs: 4.5g

Seasoning the tomato and mozzarella is the often overlooked secret to a good Caprese salad!

1 PREHEAT a grill or grill pan over medium-high heat.

2 SLICE top off eggplant and discard. Slice eggplant into 8 thick slices about ¾ inch thick. Toss eggplant slices in olive oil and lightly season with salt and pepper.

3 PLACE the eggplant slices on the hot grill and cook 3–4 minutes on each side, until dark grill marks have appeared. Remove from grill and let cool.

4 ASSEMBLE the salad by arranging first a slice of grilled eggplant, then a slice of tomato, then mozzarella, then finally basil. Repeat until you've created 8 of these stacks.

5 LIGHTLY season all with salt and pepper, then drizzle with balsamic vinegar and extra virgin olive oil just before serving.

HELPFUL TIPS

Be sure to purchase balsamic vinegar and not "glaze," as balsamic glaze contains a lot of added sugar and some even contain corn syrup.

FIVE SPICE CHICKEN SALAD

WITH CASHEWS AND APPLE

We make a lot of chicken salad in our house because we always have leftover rotisserie chicken from those nights we grab a quick dinner at the grocery store deli. This Asian-influenced chicken salad is a great twist on the classic, with five spice powder (a seasoning sold in either the spice or ethnic food aisle), roasted cashews, and crisp apple.

SHOPPING LIST

2 cups cooked chicken

⅔ cup sour cream

⅓ cup roasted cashews

¼ cup sliced celery

¼ cup diced apple

2 tablespoons sliced scallions

2 teaspoons soy sauce

1 teaspoon five spice powder

Calories: 175
Fat: 10g
Protein: 15.5g
Fiber: 0.5g
Net Carbs: 4g

1 FOLD all ingredients together in a large bowl, shredding chicken with a fork until it is at your desired consistency.

2 COVER and refrigerate for 30 minutes to allow the flavors to mingle before serving.

HELPFUL TIPS

If you are just starting out and watching your carbs very closely, simply omit the apple to take this from 4g of carbs to less than 1g per serving.

Try serving wrapped or in a "cup" made from fresh, crisp cabbage!

EASY CHEESY TURKEY BURGERS
Cheese and Veggie Stuffed Turkey Patties

Even though regular ground beef is perfectly low-carb, still like the variety of making turkey burgers from time to time (especially when ground turkey is on sale). This recipe has bell pepper, onion, and Cheddar cheese mixed throughout the meat for tons of flavor in every bite. Just remember to skip the bun and serve these platter-style!

SHOPPING LIST

Nonstick cooking spray

2½ pounds freshly ground turkey

1 cup shredded sharp
  Cheddar cheese

1 large egg

½ cup finely diced red bell pepper

¼ cup diced red onion

1 teaspoon salt

½ teaspoon poultry seasoning

¼ teaspoon black pepper

⅛ teaspoon garlic powder

Burger fixings, to serve

Calories: 275
Fat: 16.5g
Protein: 34.5g
Fiber: 0g
Net Carbs: 0.5g

1 SPRAY a large skillet with nonstick cooking spray and set aside.

2 PLACE all ingredients into a bowl and, using your hands for best results, mix well.

3 FORM the meat mix into 10 equal burger patties.

4 COOK the turkey burgers in the pan over medium-high heat for 5 minutes on each side, until completely cooked through. Serve with traditional burger toppings and fixings, as desired!

HELPFUL TIPS

These can be grilled; just make sure that the grill is preheated well and that you do not try to flip the burgers until they are well marked, or the turkey may stick to the grates.

Cooking the cheese right inside the burger patties keeps the ground turkey nice and moist.

SPINACH QUICHE

Crustless Quiche with Spinach and Swiss Cheese

Quiche is a great lunch option when you are eating low-carb, as everything except the crust is already naturally low in carbs. This "master" quiche recipe with spinach and Swiss cheese will get you on track to creating any low-carb quiche your mind can dream up!

SHOPPING LIST

Nonstick cooking spray

6 large eggs

¼ cup heavy cream

½ teaspoon minced garlic

¾ teaspoon salt

¼ teaspoon black pepper

⅛ teaspoon ground nutmeg

1 (10-ounce) bag frozen chopped spinach, thawed and drained

2 cups shredded Swiss cheese

1 tablespoon finely diced red bell pepper

Calories: 180
Fat: 13g
Protein: 13g
Fiber: 1g
Net Carbs: 2g

1 PREHEAT oven to 350°. Spray an 8-inch square baking dish or 9-inch pie pan with nonstick cooking spray.

2 WHISK together the eggs, heavy cream, garlic, salt, pepper, and nutmeg.

3 FOLD the spinach, Swiss cheese, and bell pepper into the egg mixture and then pour all into the prepared baking dish.

4 BAKE 40 minutes, or until the top of the quiche is golden brown and a toothpick inserted into it comes out mostly clean. Let cool 5 minutes before serving warm, or serve chilled, if desired.

HELPFUL TIPS

This basic quiche recipe can be used to make any low-carb quiche by switching out the type of cheese or adding proteins such as diced ham.

Though it adds a step, I love to add sautéed diced yellow onion to this as well!

Spinach and Artichoke
Deviled Eggs

Greek Dill and
Feta Dip

"Garlic Knot" Chicken Wings

APPETIZERS

SPINACH AND ARTICHOKE DEVILED EGGS
Dip Into This Unique Twist on Two Classics

I've combined two of everyone's favorite appetizers to make this wholly new way to impress your party guests. To be honest, I'm not sure why I didn't think of stuffing deviled eggs with a spinach and artichoke dip filling before, as it is just as good as it sounds!

SHOPPING LIST

8 hard-boiled eggs, peeled

3 tablespoons mayonnaise

2 teaspoons lemon juice

3 tablespoons grated
Parmesan cheese

2 tablespoons drained cooked
spinach, finely chopped

¼ teaspoon salt

⅛ teaspoon onion powder

⅛ teaspoon black pepper

8 quarters marinated
artichoke hearts

Calories: 110
Fat: 7g
Protein: 8g
Fiber: 2g
Net Carbs: 2g

1 CUT hard-boiled eggs in half, and transfer yolks to a mixing bowl.

2 ADD remaining ingredients except artichoke hearts to the mixing bowl, and mash together to make a filling.

3 STUFF all egg white halves with a heaping spoonful of the filling. Top each with a quartered artichoke heart, and serve chilled.

HELPFUL TIPS

These can also be served hot by baking (artichoke garnish included) in a 375° oven for 12–15 minutes, or until filling is bubbly hot.

For more color, add a pinch of diced roasted red peppers into the filling!

"GARLIC KNOT" CHICKEN WINGS

Crispy Baked Chicken Wings with Garlic and Parmesan

I can never have chicken wings too often; they may just be the perfect low-carb food (or I just like them a lot). When I'm not feeling like hot wings, I bake this recipe with tons of fresh garlic and Parmesan. The flavors remind me of garlic knots from a pizza parlor, hence the title.

SHOPPING LIST

2 tablespoons olive oil

2 tablespoons minced garlic

1 teaspoon garlic powder

½ teaspoon salt

½ teaspoon black pepper

3½ pounds large fresh
   chicken wings

⅓ cup grated Parmesan cheese

Calories: 280
Fat: 12.5g
Protein: 40g
Fiber: 0g
Net Carbs: 0g

1 PREHEAT oven to 375°, and line a sheet pan with aluminum foil.

2 COMBINE the olive oil, garlic, garlic powder, salt, and pepper in a bowl. Add the chicken wings and toss well to coat each piece.

3 PLACE the wings on the foil-lined baking sheet and bake for about 1 hour, or until the largest drum is cooked through and the skin is crisp.

4 IMMEDIATELY toss the cooked wings and Parmesan cheese in a bowl to coat the wings in the cheese. Serve immediately.

HELPFUL TIPS

For more zing, try skipping the Parmesan cheese, and tossing the cooked wings with 2 tablespoons each of lemon juice and melted butter!

I shop for chicken wings labeled as "jumbo" wings.

PREP TIME	COOK TIME	SERVES
15 min	30 mins	12

STUFFED JALAPEÑOS

Jalapeño Poppers Made "Open Face" Style

I love jalapeño, especially when it's roasted, as it tones down the natural heat. In this recipe, I've reinvented Cream Cheese Jalapeño Poppers by stuffing halved peppers with the cheese and baking them rather than frying. Makes 24 stuffed peppers.

SHOPPING LIST

Nonstick cooking spray

1 large egg white

8 ounces cream cheese, softened

½ teaspoon salt

¼ teaspoon onion powder

12 large fresh jalapeño peppers

Paprika

4 chives, thinly sliced

Calories: 75
Fat: 6.5g
Protein: 2g
Fiber: 0.5g
Net Carbs: 1g

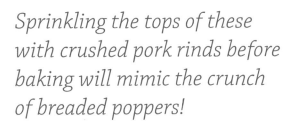

Sprinkling the tops of these with crushed pork rinds before baking will mimic the crunch of breaded poppers!

1 PREHEAT oven to 300° and spray a sheet pan with nonstick cooking spray.

2 PLACE the egg white in a mixing bowl and beat until frothy. Add the cream cheese, salt, and onion powder and fold until smooth and creamy. You can also use an electric mixer, or hand mixer to make easier work of this.

3 SLICE the jalapeños in half lengthwise and remove all seeds.

4 SPOON the cheese mixture into each of the 24 jalapeño halves, spreading to fill to the edges of the pepper. Place on the prepared sheet pan and sprinkle all with paprika for color.

5 BAKE 30 minutes before serving hot, topped with chives as garnish.

HELPFUL TIPS

For even easier cleanup, simply line the sheet pan with parchment paper or aluminum foil, though you should still spray the aluminum foil with nonstick cooking spray, as the peppers may stick.

PREP TIME	COOK TIME	SERVES
15 min	15 min	8

HOT WING BITES

Boneless Buffalo Wings with a Low-Carb Breading

I love wings, but their price has gone up quite a lot recently. On the other hand, chicken breasts are always on sale, so I invented these boneless Hot Wing Bites to "cash in" on the savings. While it may seem unconventional to bread the chicken in seasoned pork rinds, it actually replaces both the breading and the skin of traditional chicken wings.

SHOPPING LIST

4–5 cups trans-fat-free oil, for frying

4 ounces pork rinds

¼ teaspoon dry basil

¼ teaspoon dry oregano

¼ teaspoon black pepper

⅛ teaspoon garlic powder

1½ pounds boneless, skinless chicken breast, cut into 1-inch cubes

3 large eggs, beaten

¼ cup butter, melted

¼ cup Louisiana Hot Sauce

Calories: 300
Fat: 20g
Protein: 30g
Fiber: 0g
Net Carbs: 0.5g

You've got to serve this alongside blue cheese dressing for dipping!

1 ADD the frying oil to a heavy pot, leaving at least 4 inches to the top, and place over medium-high heat, or use an electric deep fryer filled to the fill line, and preheated to 350°.

2 ADD the pork rinds and dry seasonings to a large plastic food storage bag, and use a rolling pin or heavy can to crush the pork rinds into crumbs.

3 DIP the cubed chicken in the beaten eggs, then place into the plastic bag of seasoned crumbs. Shake to fully coat chicken.

4 FRY the breaded chicken in small batches for 4 minutes per batch, or until golden brown and cutting into one reveals no pink. Transfer to paper towels to drain excess oil.

5 IN a large bowl, combine the melted butter and hot sauce. Quickly toss the fried chicken pieces in the sauce to lightly coat before serving.

HELPFUL TIPS

These can also be baked rather than fried by simply placing on a greased sheet pan and baking at 400° for 12–15 minutes, or until chicken is thoroughly cooked.

ROASTED GARLIC MARINATED MUSHROOMS

IN GARLIC OIL WITH SWEET ROASTED GARLIC

For an incredible flavor, these mushrooms are marinated in Italian dressing made from the oil used to roast the garlic. Roasting the garlic makes it sweet and tender, allowing you to eat the cloves whole—and then keep eating them!

SHOPPING LIST

Cloves of 3 heads garlic, peeled

⅓ cup olive oil

16 ounces button
    mushrooms, halved

3 tablespoons red wine vinegar

1 tablespoon chopped
    fresh oregano

½ teaspoon salt

⅛ teaspoon pepper

Calories: 115
Fat: 9g
Protein: 3.5g
Fiber: 1.5g
Net Carbs: 5g

1 PREHEAT oven to 375°.

2 PLACE the garlic and olive oil in a baking dish, spreading the garlic in a single layer. Bake 20–25 minutes, flipping cloves halfway through. Garlic is roasted once it is golden brown. Remove to serving bowl. Let cool.

3 ADD the mushrooms and remaining ingredients to the cooled garlic cloves in oil. Stir to combine.

4 COVER and refrigerate at least 12 hours, to marinate. Serve chilled.

HELPFUL TIPS

You can buy jars of whole peeled garlic cloves in the produce section of the grocery store to make ridiculously easy work of the prep!

If I have any on hand, I also like to add a whole sprig of thyme to the marinade.

LOADED "FAUX-TATO" SKINS
An Ingenious Low-Carb Reinvention

I've always said that in order to not miss what we love, we need to "reinvent" what we love using natural, fresh ingredients. Now, who doesn't love loaded potato skins? What we really love about potato skins is the toppings, and yellow squash makes the perfect low-carb alternative for those same toppings.

SHOPPING LIST

Nonstick cooking spray

3 medium yellow squash

Salt and pepper

⅛ teaspoon garlic powder

⅛ teaspoon onion powder

½ cup shredded Cheddar cheese

3 strips cooked bacon, crumbled

¼ cup sour cream

1 scallion, thinly sliced

Calories: 55
Fat: 4g
Protein: 3g
Fiber: 0.5g
Net Carbs: 1.5g

1 PREHEAT oven to 375°, and spray a sheet pan with nonstick cooking spray.

2 TRIM the ends off the squash, cut each in half lengthwise, and place cut side up on the prepared pan.

3 GENEROUSLY season the squash with salt and pepper, then with garlic powder and onion powder.

4 TOP each seasoned squash half with an even amount of the Cheddar cheese and crumbled bacon.

5 BAKE for 12 minutes, or until cheese is bubbly and squash is tender. Serve with a dollop of sour cream and sliced scallions on top.

HELPFUL TIPS

Line your sheet pan with parchment paper or aluminum foil to catch any runaway shreds of cheese and make cleanup a breeze.

Zucchini can be used in place of the yellow squash, if desired (or if they look fresher).

BALSAMIC & BASIL VEGGIE KEBABS
Summer Vegetables, Scrumptiously Skewered

I love grilled vegetables of all kinds, but they aren't the easiest things to keep from falling between the grates of the grill—that's where kebabs like these come in; they not only hold things together, but make for a far nicer presentation at the table.

SHOPPING LIST

Bamboo skewers

2 large yellow squash

2 large zucchini

1 red onion

16 cherry or grape tomatoes

1 red bell pepper

1 yellow bell pepper (may use green)

½ teaspoon kosher salt

½ teaspoon black pepper

½ teaspoon minced garlic

¼ cup extra virgin olive oil

¼ cup balsamic vinegar

2 tablespoons chopped fresh basil

Calories: 80
Fat: 4g
Protein: 2.5g
Fiber: 3g
Net Carbs: 5g

If you don't have balsamic vinegar, red wine vinegar may be used in its place, and it's slightly lower in carbs, too!

1   SOAK the bamboo skewers in water for 30 minutes to keep them from scorching on the grill.

2   PREHEAT a grill to medium high, or heat an indoor grill pan on high heat.

3   CUT ends from vegetables, clean the seeds out of the peppers, then slice all vegetables into 2-inch pieces, leaving the cherry tomatoes whole.

4   ADD the cut vegetables to a bowl, and toss with salt, pepper, garlic, and olive oil.

5   THREAD alternating pieces of all the vegetables on each skewer, leaving about 2 inches of clean skewer at the bottom of each kebab.

6   PLACE the kebabs on the edges of the grill (where it is less hot), and cook about 2 minutes on each of the 4 sides. They are done when they have been "marked" by the grill on all sides. Drizzle with balsamic vinegar, and sprinkle with chopped basil before serving.

HELPFUL TIPS

The key to making good kebabs is to cut the vegetables into pieces that are close to equal in size; this way they will all cook evenly.

FRESH GUACAMOLE

Ditch the Preservatives and Eat Fresh

The best guacamole is the simplest and freshest made from the fewest ingredients and perfectly ripe avocados. There are plenty of store-bought options on the market now, but I've found that they're either full of preservatives or completely devoid of any flavor. While you've got to let the avocado shine, you still need a little lime, onion, and cilantro to balance things out.

SHOPPING LIST

2 ripe Hass avocados

⅓ cup sour cream

2 tablespoons minced red onion

1 teaspoon minced garlic

Juice of ½ lime

2 tablespoons finely chopped cilantro

¼ teaspoon salt

⅛ teaspoon pepper

Calories: 125
Fat: 12g
Protein: 1.5g
Fiber: 3.5g
Net Carbs: 1.5g

1   HALVE the avocados and remove pits, discarding.

2   USE a spoon to scoop the avocado pulp out of the skin and into a mixing bowl, then mash the pulp with a fork until almost smooth.

3   FOLD in remaining ingredients and serve. Cover and refrigerate for at least 1 hour for an even better flavor.

HELPFUL TIPS

The sour cream in this can be omitted entirely, though I like to add it to up the creaminess of the finished guacamole.

Try my Baked Zucchini Chips (page 180), for dipping! Or serve alongside southwestern entrées.

ASIAN PORK MEATBALLS
In a Light and Savory Orange Zest Sauce

These Asian Pork Meatballs are nothing like the sweet and sour type meatballs with pineapple you may have had at a potluck, and that is a very good thing! Those are swimming in sugar, while these are drizzled in a more savory sauce with the flavor of a Chinese pork dumpling appetizer.

SHOPPING LIST

MEATBALLS

1 pound lean ground pork

1 large egg

¼ cup finely minced scallions

1 tablespoon soy sauce

1 teaspoon minced ginger, or ¼ teaspoon ground

SAUCE

1 tablespoon sesame oil

2 tablespoons soy sauce

2 tablespoons water

1 teaspoon cider vinegar

½ teaspoon sugar substitute, optional

½ teaspoon finely grated orange zest

Calories: 210
Fat: 16g
Protein: 15g
Fiber: 0g
Net Carbs: 1.5g

1 COMBINE all Meatball ingredients in a large mixing bowl. Use your hands to mix and then form into golf ball-sized meatballs.

2 PLACE sesame oil in a skillet over medium-high heat. Once hot, add meatballs and brown well on all sides, about 8 minutes.

3 WHISK together remaining Sauce ingredients and add to the skillet. Reduce heat to a simmer and let meatballs simmer 5 minutes, stirring occasionally.

4 SERVE drizzled in the juices from the pan.

HELPFUL TIPS

I like to use lean ground pork in these as regular ground pork releases a lot of grease into the pan, diluting the sauce.

Garnish these with additional sliced scallions or with toasted sesame seeds.

BALTIMORE BAKED CRAB DIP

CREAMY CRAB DIP WITH CHEDDAR AND OLD BAY SEASONING

This is one of my oldest low-carb recipes and one that we've made dozens of times over the years. As a chef's work is never done, I've tweaked the recipe to perfection and the result is a creamy crab dip that tastes like it is straight off a Baltimore boardwalk.

SHOPPING LIST

Nonstick cooking spray

8 ounces cream cheese, softened

8 ounces lump crabmeat

1 cup shredded sharp
   Cheddar cheese

½ cup sour cream

2 tablespoons sliced scallions

1 teaspoon Old Bay Seasoning

¼ teaspoon black pepper

⅛ teaspoon garlic powder

Calories: 230
Fat: 20g
Protein: 14g
Fiber: 0g
Net Carbs: 2g

1 PLACE rack in center position and preheat oven to 350°. Spray an 8-inch baking dish with nonstick cooking spray.

2 ADD all ingredients to a mixing bowl and fold together. Spread into the greased baking dish and sprinkle with additional Old Bay Seasoning to add color, if desired.

3 BAKE 25 minutes, until bubbly and beginning to brown. Serve immediately.

HELPFUL TIPS

This is great with sliced vegetables or my Rosemary Flax Crackers (page 179), for dipping.

I like to add a tablespoon of chopped roasted red pepper into this for even more color.

ITALIAN SAUSAGE STUFFED MUSHROOMS
THE OFFICIAL MUSHROOM OF ITALY (NOT REALLY)

Stuffed mushrooms are better when they are made low-carb; there's just no doubt about it. Why stuff them full of flavorless breadcrumbs when you can make a creamy filling out of Italian sausage and Parmesan cheese as I have in this recipe?

SHOPPING LIST

Nonstick cooking spray

16 button mushrooms

¼ pound ground Italian sausage, without casings

1 teaspoon minced garlic

1 tablespoon minced red onion

2 ounces cream cheese

2 tablespoons grated Parmesan cheese

1 tablespoon finely diced roasted red pepper

⅛ teaspoon salt

⅛ teaspoon pepper

Calories: 95
Fat: 7g
Protein: 6g
Fiber: 0.5g
Net Carbs: 1.5g

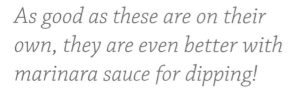

As good as these are on their own, they are even better with marinara sauce for dipping!

1 PREHEAT oven to 350°, and spray a sheet pan with nonstick cooking spray.

2 CLEAN mushrooms, and remove stems by twisting, placing mushroom caps on the sheet pan as you work. Chop mushroom stems and set aside.

3 HEAT sausage in a skillet over medium-high heat until well browned and crumbled. Add the chopped mushroom stems, garlic, and red onion, and sauté for 1 minute. Drain excess grease.

4 ADD cream cheese, Parmesan cheese, roasted red pepper, salt, and pepper to the skillet, and stir until all is combined into a filling.

5 STUFF each mushroom cap with a heaping spoonful of the filling. Bake the stuffed mushrooms for 15–20 minutes, or until mushrooms are tender. Serve hot.

HELPFUL TIPS

I am all about cooking with color, so try garnishing these with chopped fresh flat-leaf parsley to give them a nice touch of green!

GREEK DILL AND FETA DIP
GOES PERFECTLY WITH SLICED CUCUMBERS

I got the idea for this dip when Rachel brought home Greek yogurt and cucumbers to make tzatziki sauce. I thought it would be interesting to "deconstruct" the flavors of tzatziki and use the cucumbers as chips to dip, and the results were even better than I expected!

SHOPPING LIST

16 ounces plain Greek yogurt

4 ounces crumbled feta cheese

2 tablespoons chopped fresh dill

1 tablespoon minced red onion

2 teaspoons minced garlic

¼ teaspoon black pepper

¼ teaspoon salt

Sliced cucumbers, for dipping

Calories: 70
Fat: 3g
Protein: 8g
Fiber: 0g
Net Carbs: 2.5g

1 ADD all of the ingredients, except the sliced cucumbers, to a mixing or serving bowl and fold together.

2 CHILL for at least 1 hour before serving to let the flavors combine. Stir before serving alongside sliced cucumbers, for dipping.

HELPFUL TIPS

You can also make my Rosemary Flax Crackers (page 179), for dipping. Substitute 1 teaspoon of dried oregano in place of the fresh rosemary for crackers that better complement the Greek flavors in this dip.

Be sure to purchase "plain" Greek yogurt and not "vanilla" yogurt, or you'll find yourself making the strangest dessert anyone has ever had.

Teriyaki & Ginger Chicken Thighs

Chimichurri Chicken
Breasts

Chicken with Lemon
and Artichokes

POULTRY

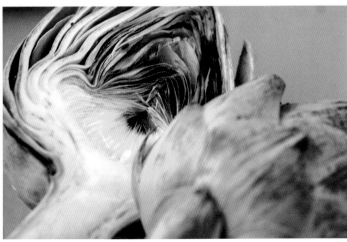

PREP TIME	COOK TIME	SERVES
20 min	6 min	4

CHICKEN WITH LEMON AND ARTICHOKES

LIKE CHICKEN PICCATA, ONLY BETTER!

This recipe of chicken in a lemon butter sauce with capers is a lot like the classic chicken piccata, only made even better with the addition of sweet red onion and tender artichoke hearts.

SHOPPING LIST

1 tablespoon olive oil

4 boneless, skinless chicken breasts

Salt and pepper

3 tablespoons diced red onion

1 teaspoon minced garlic

Juice of 1 lemon

⅓ cup chicken broth

⅔ cup quartered artichoke hearts, canned or jarred, drained

1 tablespoon capers, drained

2 tablespoons butter

Calories: 295
Fat: 11g
Protein: 47g
Fiber: 1.5g
Net Carbs: 2.5g

1 PLACE oil in a large sauté pan over medium-high heat.

2 ONCE the oil is hot, generously season the chicken with salt and pepper and add to the pan, cooking 4 minutes on each side.

3 ADD the red onion and garlic and cook 1 additional minute before adding lemon juice and chicken broth. Let simmer 1 minute.

4 REMOVE from heat and stir in artichoke hearts, capers, and butter. Season the sauce with salt and pepper to taste before serving.

HELPFUL TIPS

I prefer to use marinated artichoke hearts that come in a jar (instead of canned artichokes) when I'm cooking, but I usually rinse them to remove excess marinade.

A small splash of white wine goes great in the sauce as well.

CHICKEN MARSALA

AN ITALIAN CLASSIC WITHOUT THE CARBS

Chicken Marsala, prepared the traditional way, is entirely low-carb as long as you skip one little step—breading the chicken. My recipe does just that, but the mushroom and red wine sauce is so robust that you can't possibly feel like this is missing anything.

SHOPPING LIST

1 tablespoon vegetable oil

4 boneless, skinless chicken breasts

Salt and pepper

1 tablespoon butter

8 ounces baby bella mushrooms, quartered

¼ cup diced red onion

1 teaspoon minced garlic

¼ cup Marsala wine

½ cup heavy cream

1 teaspoon beef base

¼ teaspoon black pepper

1 tablespoon chopped fresh parsley

Calories: 460
Fat: 24.5g
Protein: 51g
Fiber: 1g
Net Carbs: 3.5g

When shopping for Marsala wine, "Cream Marsala" is the best for cooking.

1 HEAT vegetable oil in a large sauté pan over medium-high heat.

2 GENEROUSLY season chicken breasts with salt and pepper and add to the hot pan, cooking 4 minutes on each side, or until slicing into the thickest piece reveals no pink. Remove and set aside chicken.

3 TO the same pan, add butter and mushrooms and sauté until mushrooms begin to brown. Stir in onion and garlic and continue cooking 1 minute.

4 DEGLAZE the pan with the Marsala wine, and then stir in heavy cream, beef base, pepper, and parsley. Let simmer 4 minutes, or until liquid has reduced by about half.

5 RETURN chicken to the hot sauce before serving.

HELPFUL TIPS

Beef base is sold in small jars near the bouillon cubes in the grocery store. Not only is it less processed than bouillon cubes, it contains less salt and more flavor. In a pinch, you can substitute 1 bouillon cube in this recipe.

TRADITIONAL CHICKEN CACCIATORE
Rustic Chicken in a Hearty Tomato Sauce

This recipe for Chicken Cacciatore is made in the traditional way of braising in the sauce of tomatoes, bell pepper, onion, and Italian aromatics. The best part is that you end up with an extremely complex dish made in only one skillet!

SHOPPING LIST

2 tablespoons olive oil

4 chicken leg quarters

Salt and pepper

1 green bell pepper, chopped

½ red onion, chopped

2 teaspoons minced garlic

1 (15-ounce) can diced tomatoes

1 tablespoon balsamic vinegar

1 tablespoon chopped fresh Italian parsley

1½ teaspoons Italian seasoning

¼ teaspoon crushed red pepper flakes

8 ounces button mushrooms, quartered

Calories: 490
Fat: 31g
Protein: 45g
Fiber: 3g
Net Carbs: 5g

1 HEAT oil in a large skillet or Dutch oven over medium-high heat.

2 GENEROUSLY season chicken with salt and pepper and add to the skillet, browning the skin well. Remove chicken from pan and set aside.

3 ADD bell pepper, onion, and garlic to the skillet and sauté 2 minutes. Add the diced tomatoes and liquid from the can, balsamic vinegar, parsley, Italian seasoning, and red pepper flakes and stir.

4 RETURN chicken to the skillet, lower heat to a simmer, and cover skillet. Let simmer 30 minutes.

5 UNCOVER and add mushrooms. Let simmer an additional 15 minutes uncovered before seasoning sauce with salt and pepper to taste and serving garnished with additional fresh parsley.

HELPFUL TIPS

Any chicken pieces, with or without skin can be used in place of the chicken leg quarters in this recipe.

We like to serve this alongside spaghetti squash for a full Italian meal.

CILANTRO LIME CHICKEN THIGHS
You'll Be South of the Border of Your Kitchen

Cilantro and lime are a classic combination of Mexican flavors that really shine in the marinade for these chicken thighs. Serve them with my Southwestern Cauliflower Rice (page 166), and you'll have a meal fit for a fiesta!

SHOPPING LIST

2 tablespoons olive oil

2 tablespoons minced red onion

2 tablespoons chopped cilantro

1 teaspoon salt

1 teaspoon minced fresh garlic

½ teaspoon black pepper

Juice of 1 lime

2 pounds boneless, skinless chicken thighs

Calories: 320
Fat: 14g
Protein: 45g
Fiber: 0g
Net Carbs: 1g

1 PREHEAT oven to 400°, and line a sheet pan with aluminum foil.

2 COMBINE the olive oil, red onion, cilantro, salt, garlic, pepper, and lime juice in a bowl. Add the chicken and toss well, coating each piece. Let marinate 15 minutes.

3 PLACE the marinated chicken on the foil-lined baking sheet and bake for 35–40 minutes, or until the largest piece is cooked through or a meat thermometer inserted into the thickest part reads 165°.

4 SERVE with lime wedges to squeeze over the chicken.

HELPFUL TIPS

Add a pinch of ground cayenne pepper to the marinade if you like a little heat.

We also like to serve these topped with sliced avocado!

TERIYAKI & GINGER CHICKEN THIGHS
ASIAN–STYLE CHICKEN, GINGERLY MARINATED

Ask any chef what part of the chicken they like best and I bet they'll all say the chicken thigh! Okay, we like wings, too! Chicken thighs stay moist and beautifully absorb flavors, such as the classic Asian flavors of the teriyaki and ginger marinade in this recipe.

SHOPPING LIST

MARINADE

15 ounces teriyaki sauce

¼ cup sesame oil

1 tablespoon minced ginger

1 teaspoon minced garlic

2 tablespoons lemon juice

1 tablespoon sugar substitute

CHICKEN

2 pounds boneless, skinless
   chicken thighs

1 tablespoon sesame seeds, toasted

Calories: 330
Fat: 15g
Protein: 45g
Fiber: 0g
Net Carbs: 2g

1 COMBINE all Marinade ingredients in a large mixing bowl.

2 ADD the chicken to the marinade, cover, and shake gently to mix. Refrigerate for at least 2 hours.

3 ONCE marinated, preheat oven to 400°, and line a sheet pan with aluminum foil.

4 PLACE the chicken on the foil-lined sheet pan and bake for 35–40 minutes, or until cutting into the largest piece reveals no opaque meat.

5 SERVE garnished with toasted sesame seeds.

HELPFUL TIPS

To toast sesame seeds, heat a small skillet until hot. Add the raw seeds and stir until they start to brown and pop. Remove from heat and cool.

Look for a teriyaki sauce with the consistency of soy sauce, not a thick and sugary marinade.

SWEDISH TURKEY MEATBALLS
It's Like There's a Turkey Loose at IKEA

Swedish meatballs are a staple in many households, and have always been one in ours—however, far too many people rely on frozen meatballs to make this dish. Frozen meatballs are not only stuffed with "filler" ingredients, but are almost always seasoned with Italian seasonings that aren't suitable for this "Swedish" dish.

SHOPPING LIST

MEATBALLS

1 pound ground turkey

1 large egg

¼ cup finely minced onion

1 tablespoon chopped Italian parsley

½ teaspoon salt

¼ teaspoon pepper

¼ teaspoon allspice

SAUCE

2 tablespoons butter

½ cup water

1 teaspoon beef base

8 ounces sour cream

½ teaspoon onion powder

¼ teaspoon pepper

Calories: 405
Fat: 30g
Protein: 34.5g
Fiber: 0g
Net Carbs: 3g

1 COMBINE all Meatball ingredients in a large mixing bowl. Use your hands to mix and then form into golf ball-sized meatballs.

2 PLACE butter in a skillet over medium-high heat. Once sizzling, add meatballs and brown well on all sides, about 8 minutes.

3 ADD the water and beef base and let simmer 5 minutes, or until water has reduced by about half.

4 REMOVE from heat and stir in sour cream, onion powder, and pepper before serving garnished with chopped parsley, if desired.

HELPFUL TIPS

Beef base is sold in small jars near the bouillon cubes in the grocery store. Not only is it less processed than bouillon cubes, it contains less salt and more flavor. In a pinch, you can substitute 1 bouillon cube in this recipe.

Ground beef can be used for regular Swedish meatballs if turkey isn't for you.

CLASSIC PESTO CHICKEN
with Toasted Pine Nuts, Basil, and Parmesan

Pesto is a simple classic that too many people purchase in jars. I've tried the jarred stuff and you can barely taste the basil and there's not even a hint of real pine nuts to be found. It's just another instance in which cooking with fresh foods is most certainly best.

SHOPPING LIST

4 boneless, skinless chicken breasts

PESTO SAUCE

¼ cup pine nuts

¼ cup olive oil

1 clove garlic

¾ packed cup basil

⅓ cup grated Parmesan cheese

¼ teaspoon salt

¼ teaspoon pepper

Calories: 385
Fat: 22g
Protein: 46g
Fiber: 0g
Net Carbs: 1.5g

1 PREHEAT oven to 375° and line a sheet pan with parchment paper.

2 START the Pesto Sauce by placing the pine nuts on the lined sheet pan and baking 8–10 minutes, just until golden brown. Leave oven on to cook the chicken.

3 PLACE the toasted pine nuts in a food processor and add remaining Pesto Sauce ingredients, pulsing until well chopped and almost smooth.

4 PLACE chicken breasts on the sheet pan and spread each with an equal amount of the Pesto Sauce.

5 BAKE 25–30 minutes, or until slicing into the thickest piece reveals no pink. Serve immediately.

HELPFUL TIPS

If the pesto mixture is too thick, simply add additional olive oil until it is a smooth paste.

Pesto can also be made with walnuts or almonds in place of the more expensive pine nuts.

CHIMICHURRI CHICKEN BREASTS

GRILLED CHICKEN MARINATED IN A FRESH HERB SAUCE

Chimichurri is a parsley and garlic sauce from Argentina that is usually served with steak, but makes an absolutely great marinade (and sauce) for any grilled meat. Personally, I prefer it on chicken, as it is in this recipe.

SHOPPING LIST

4 boneless, skinless chicken breasts

1 packed cup flat-leaf parsley

1½ tablespoons minced garlic

1 tablespoon diced red onion

¼ cup olive oil

2 tablespoons red wine vinegar

1 teaspoon dried oregano

½ teaspoon salt

¼ teaspoon pepper

Calories: 405
Fat: 21g
Protein: 50g
Fiber: 0.5g
Net Carbs: 1g

This goes great with my Summer Squash Sauté (page 155).

1 PLACE the chicken breasts in a food storage bag or plastic container.

2 IN a food processor or blender, pulse remaining ingredients to create the chimichurri sauce.

3 PLACE half of the chimichurri sauce (reserve the remaining sauce to top the cooked chicken) in the storage container with the chicken. Cover and shake to coat chicken evenly. Refrigerate for 2 hours to marinate.

4 ONCE chicken is marinated, preheat a grill or indoor grill pan on high. Remove chicken from marinade and discard the used marinade.

5 PLACE the chicken breasts on the grill and cook 8–10 minutes on each side, or until slicing into the thickest part reveals no pink.

6 SERVE topped with additional chimichurri sauce.

HELPFUL TIPS

Adding 2 tablespoons of fresh oregano leaves to the sauce makes this even better, though I like to keep the dried in it as well for more flavor.

JERK CHICKEN LEGS
A Little Spice, A Lot of Flavor

I've been cooking Caribbean-style food for decades—we actually called it "Floribbean" cuisine down in south Florida! Jerk chicken is a staple in south Florida, but I don't see why it isn't a staple everywhere.

SHOPPING LIST

4 chicken leg quarters

MARINADE

2 tablespoons olive oil

Juice of 1 lime

2 teaspoons minced garlic

2 teaspoons dried thyme

2 teaspoons allspice

1 teaspoon onion powder

1 teaspoon sugar
    substitute, optional

¾ teaspoon salt

½ teaspoon black pepper

¼ teaspoon ground cayenne pepper

Calories: 440
Fat: 30g
Protein: 42.5g
Fiber: 0g
Net Carbs: 1.5g

1 COMBINE all Marinade ingredients and rub onto chicken leg quarters. Cover and refrigerate 1 hour to marinate.

2 PREHEAT oven to 450° and place marinated chicken on a sheet pan.

3 BAKE 30 minutes, flipping chicken halfway through. Slice into the thickest piece to test for doneness before serving.

HELPFUL TIPS

This is extremely good when served alongside sliced fresh cantaloupe or honeydew to balance the spice of the chicken. Or dice melon and red onion and season with salt and pepper to make a quick salsa.

This goes perfectly with my Southwestern Cauliflower Rice (page 166).

SMOTHERED CHICKEN CORDON BLEU
with "Honey" Mustard Sauce

While this Smothered Chicken Cordon Bleu is anything but traditional, I can say that it has many of the same flavors of the original while taking far, far less effort to prepare. It's a real family-pleasing dish!

SHOPPING LIST

1 tablespoon butter

1 tablespoon vegetable oil

4 boneless, skinless chicken breasts

Salt and pepper

Paprika

4 thick slices deli ham

4 slices Swiss cheese

HONEY MUSTARD SAUCE

¼ cup heavy cream

1 tablespoon yellow mustard

1 teaspoon sugar substitute

1 teaspoon parsley flakes

Calories: 355
Fat: 20.5g
Protein: 38.5g
Fiber: 0.5g
Net Carbs: 2.5g

This is the easiest "Cordon Bleu" you can make!

1   HEAT butter and vegetable oil in a large sauté pan over medium-high heat.

2   GENEROUSLY season chicken breasts with salt, pepper, and paprika and add to the hot pan, cooking 4 minutes on each side, or until slicing into the thickest piece reveals no pink. Transfer chicken to a broiler or sheet pan.

3   PLACE oven rack 6 inches from the top and preheat broiler to high.

4   FOLD each slice of ham and place atop each chicken breast. Top ham with a slice of Swiss cheese. Place topped chicken under broiler and broil only 2 minutes, until cheese is hot and bubbly.

5   MAKE the Honey Mustard Sauce by combining all ingredients in a small sauce pot over medium heat and bringing up to a simmer. Let simmer until the mixture has reduced by about half. Serve drizzled over the smothered chicken.

HELPFUL TIPS

I like to add a teaspoon of coarsely ground mustard into the mustard sauce to add a little texture, but Dijon is only recommended if you like spice!

ARUGULA CHICKEN PINWHEELS
WITH GOAT CHEESE AND ROASTED RED PEPPER

Arugula, goat cheese, and roasted red peppers make for beautiful (and delicious!) layers in these baked chicken breast roll-ups. These are technically "roulades," and though I've used that term elsewhere in the book, I thought I'd call these pinwheels because I think they are too good to scare people away with such a technical title!

SHOPPING LIST

Nonstick cooking spray

4 small boneless, skinless chicken breasts

Salt and pepper

¼ teaspoon garlic powder

4 ounces goat cheese

1 cup arugula

⅓ cup sliced roasted red pepper

¼ teaspoon dried oregano

Calories: 280
Fat: 11.5g
Protein: 41.5g
Fiber: 0g
Net Carbs: 1.5g

I buy jars of whole roasted red peppers and slice them myself, as jars of the sliced variety are sliced quite thin.

1 PREHEAT oven to 400° and spray a sheet pan with nonstick cooking spray.

2 USING a meat mallet, pound the chicken breasts out until about ⅓ inch thick at all parts. Season both sides of each breast with salt and pepper and then sprinkle with the garlic powder.

3 THINLY slice or break the goat cheese into small pieces and distribute evenly over the 4 chicken breasts. Evenly layer arugula and then roasted red peppers over the goat cheese.

4 ROLL each chicken breast up, starting on the short end, until chicken is overlapping and you have long roulades. Use toothpicks or tie with baking twine to ensure they keep their shape.

5 SPRINKLE the rolled chicken with dried oregano and bake 20 minutes, or until slicing into the largest roulade reveals no pink. Let cool 5 minutes before slicing each breast to serve.

HELPFUL TIPS

You want to really layer on the arugula, about 3 leaves thick across the surface. It will look like a lot more than you need, but remember that it cooks down in the same way spinach does.

PARMESAN CRUSTED CHICKEN BREASTS
TENDER CHICKEN WITH A CREAMY PARMESAN TOPPING

Warming up mayonnaise makes it almost identical to the classic French béarnaise sauce. By adding Parmesan cheese to the mayonnaise, it actually bubbles up and browns, making it a deliciously perfect topping for the chicken breasts in this recipe.

SHOPPING LIST

Nonstick cooking spray

4 boneless, skinless chicken breasts

1 tablespoon olive oil

½ teaspoon salt

⅛ teaspoon black pepper

¼ cup grated Parmesan cheese

2 tablespoons mayonnaise

1 teaspoon Italian seasoning

Calories: 405
Fat: 15g
Protein: 64g
Fiber: 0g
Net Carbs: 1g

1 PREHEAT oven to 375°, and spray a baking sheet with nonstick cooking spray.

2 PLACE the chicken on the baking sheet, drizzle with the olive oil, and generously season with salt and pepper.

3 ADD remaining ingredients to a small bowl and mix well. Top the chicken breasts with an even amount of the mixture, and spread to coat.

4 BAKE for 35–40 minutes, or until cooked through, and slicing into the thickest piece reveals no pink, or a meat thermometer registers 165°. Serve immediately.

5 REMOVE the chicken from the oven and serve hot, garnished with fresh basil or oregano, if desired!

HELPFUL TIPS

You can use this same simple Parmesan and mayo crust to top tilapia or shrimp by lowering the baking time to 12–15 minutes.

For even more flavor, drizzle the chicken breasts with a little fresh lemon juice before topping with the Parmesan sauce.

CHILI RUBBED CHICKEN BREASTS

CHICKEN WITH A SLIGHTLY SPICY CHILI RUB

I love making rubs to bake or grill chicken, as they encapsulate the meat with flavor—in this case, the great southwestern flavors of chili and cumin. Squeezing fresh lime over the cooked chicken is an absolute must, as it really brightens things up.

SHOPPING LIST

4 boneless, skinless chicken breasts

Fresh lime wedges

CHILI RUB

1½ tablespoons olive oil

2 tablespoons chopped cilantro

1 tablespoon chili powder

1 tablespoon ground cumin

1 teaspoon minced garlic

1 teaspoon salt

½ teaspoon black pepper

⅛ teaspoon cayenne pepper

Calories: 250
Fat: 7.5g
Protein: 46g
Fiber: 1g
Net Carbs: 1g

1 PREHEAT oven to 400°, and line a sheet pan with aluminum foil.

2 COMBINE all Chili Rub ingredients and rub into the chicken breasts.

3 PLACE the rubbed chicken on prepared sheet pan and bake 20 minutes, or until cutting into the thickest piece reveals no pink.

4 SERVE with fresh lime wedges to squeeze over top.

HELPFUL TIPS

If you top these with a handful of diced red onion and diced tomato before baking and then top with Cheddar-Jack cheese when they are hot out of the oven, you've got a recipe I call Easy Cheesy Chili Chicken.

This goes great with a dollop of my Fresh Guacamole (page 77)!

HERB ROASTED FAMILY-STYLE CHICKEN
As Simple As it Gets

This is my absolute master recipe for roasting chicken. The meat falls right off the bones and is flavored by wonderfully aromatic fresh herbs. My secret is, you don't roast the chicken whole, but split into pieces (breasts, thighs, wings, and legs). While it may take 2 hours to roast, getting these same tender results with a whole chicken would take far, far longer.

SHOPPING LIST

Nonstick cooking spray

1 whole chicken, separated into 8 pieces

1 tablespoon chopped fresh thyme leaves

1 tablespoon chopped fresh oregano

1 tablespoon chopped fresh Italian parsley

1 teaspoon kosher salt

1 teaspoon paprika

½ teaspoon pepper

½ teaspoon poultry seasoning

Juice of ½ lemon

Calories: 305
Fat: 13g
Protein: 43g
Fiber: 0g
Net Carbs: 1g

1 PREHEAT oven to 350° and spray a roasting pan with nonstick cooking spray.

2 PLACE the chicken pieces evenly throughout the pan and sprinkle all herbs and seasonings over top each piece.

3 DRIZZLE lemon juice over the chicken and then cover pan with aluminum foil. Bake 1 hour.

4 UNCOVER and baste with the drippings from the pan. Continue baking uncovered 1 additional hour. The chicken should be browned and falling off the bones. Serve garnished with additional chopped parsley.

HELPFUL TIPS

Sliced yellow squash and zucchini can be added to the roasting pan in the last 40 minutes to bake alongside the chicken and make this into a complete meal.

Any combination of fresh herbs can be used to prepare this recipe.

CREAMY CHICKEN AND SWEET POTATO CURRY

Complex Indian Flavors, Made Easy

In this dish, the strong flavor of curry is counterbalanced with cream and sweet potato, for a chicken dinner that is anything but ordinary.

SHOPPING LIST

1 large sweet potato, thinly sliced

1 tablespoon vegetable oil

1 tablespoon butter

2 pounds boneless, skinless chicken breasts, sliced into 1-inch thick strips

Salt and pepper

1 teaspoon minced garlic

1½ teaspoons curry powder

1 cup chicken broth

1 teaspoon cider vinegar

½ cup heavy cream

5 scallions, sliced into 1-inch lengths

Calories: 375
Fat: 14.5g
Protein: 55g
Fiber: 2g
Net Carbs: 6.5g

1 BLANCH sliced sweet potato in boiling water for 4 minutes, or until almost tender. Drain and set aside.

2 HEAT vegetable oil and butter in a large sauté pan over medium-high heat.

3 GENEROUSLY season chicken breast strips with salt and pepper and add to the hot pan, cooking until they begin to brown.

4 ADD garlic and curry powder and sauté 1 minute before adding the blanched sweet potato slices, chicken broth, vinegar, and heavy cream.

5 LET simmer 4 minutes, or until liquid has reduced by about half. Stir in scallions, season the sauce with salt to taste, and serve.

HELPFUL TIPS

This dish is best served over or alongside steamed or roasted cauliflower. Or you can mix thawed frozen cauliflower directly into the sauce before simmering in the last step.

For a very spicy curry, add a chopped jalapeño pepper, with the seeds, in step 4.

REUBEN CHICKEN ROULADES

WITH THOUSAND ISLAND SAUCE

This recipe combines two of my absolute favorite things, chicken roulades (stuffed chicken pinwheels), and a Reuben sandwich! While it may seem a little strange at first, it's actually just a variation on the classic chicken cordon bleu, with corned beef in place of ham, and sauerkraut added for crunch!

SHOPPING LIST

Nonstick cooking spray

4 small boneless, skinless chicken breasts

Salt and pepper

4 slices deli corned beef

4 slices Swiss cheese

1 cup sauerkraut, well drained

¼ cup heavy cream

1 tablespoon tomato paste

1 tablespoon finely diced cucumber

1 teaspoon sugar substitute

Calories: 385
Fat: 19.5g
Protein: 46g
Fiber: 1g
Net Carbs: 2.5g

Sprinkle the chicken with ground caraway seeds before baking to add the flavor of rye bread!

1 PREHEAT oven to 400°, and spray a sheet pan with nonstick cooking spray.

2 USING a meat mallet, pound the chicken breasts out until about ⅓ inch thick at all parts. Season both sides of each breast with salt and pepper.

3 PLACE 1 slice of corned beef and 1 slice of Swiss cheese on each chicken breast, folding to match the shape of the chicken. Disperse the sauerkraut equally over each breast.

4 ROLL each chicken breast up, starting on the short end, until chicken is overlapping and you have long roulades. Use toothpicks to ensure they keep their shape.

5 BAKE 20 minutes, or until slicing into the largest roulade reveals no pink.

6 MEANWHILE, combine heavy cream, tomato paste, cucumber, and sugar substitute to make the Thousand Island Sauce. Serve drizzled over the baked roulades.

HELPFUL TIPS

Most stores now sell "no-sugar-added" relish that can be used in place of the cucumber and sugar substitute to make the sauce.

Boneless Barbecue Ribs

Braised Short Ribs

Pork Tenderloin with Mustard Gravy

MEATS

MARINARA & MOZZARELLA MEATLOAF

Meatloaf, Made "Parmesan" Style

Lately, some of my posts on Facebook have been receiving hundreds of thousands of views, and this recipe was the single most popular post I ever made! People just can't get enough of this meatloaf topped with marinara sauce and mozzarella cheese and baked like Chicken Parmesan.

SHOPPING LIST

2 pounds lean ground beef

1½ cups marinara sauce, divided

¼ cup diced red onion

2 large eggs

½ cup grated Parmesan cheese

1½ teaspoons Italian seasoning

2 teaspoons minced garlic

½ teaspoon onion powder

¾ teaspoon salt

½ teaspoon black pepper

¾ cup mozzarella cheese

Calories: 410
Fat: 28g
Protein: 28g
Fiber: 1g
Net Carbs: 6.5g

By replacing the breadcrumbs in the meatloaf with Parmesan cheese, I've cut the carbs AND added flavor.

1 PREHEAT oven to 350°, and ready a nonstick 9x5-inch loaf pan for baking. (Or spray a regular loaf pan with nonstick cooking spray.)

2 IN a large bowl, mix the ground beef, 1 cup of the marinara sauce, diced red onion, eggs, Parmesan cheese, Italian seasoning, garlic, onion powder, salt, and pepper. (This is easiest done with your hands.)

3 EVENLY fill loaf pan with the meatloaf mixture, patting with your hands to form an even top. Bake uncovered for 45 minutes.

4 REMOVE loaf from oven and spread with remaining ½ cup of marinara sauce, and then the mozzarella cheese over the top. Return to oven and bake an additional 30 minutes, or until a meat thermometer registers 165°. Drain fat from pan and let rest 10 minutes before cutting into 8 equal slices.

HELPFUL TIPS

When shopping for marinara sauce, make sure you read the labels! While tomatoes contain some natural sugars, check the ingredients list for any added sugar or corn syrup.

PREP TIME
20 min

COOK TIME
3 hours

SERVES
6

CORNED BEEF WITH BARBECUE BRAISED CABBAGE
Will Have You Wondering Why You Ever Boiled Cabbage

This recipe takes the classic combination of corned beef and cabbage and combines it with another classic: braised cabbage. The sweet barbecue sauce caramelizes the cabbage, making for the perfect side for the salty corned beef.

SHOPPING LIST

1 corned beef brisket (about 3 pounds)

1 tablespoon butter

1 small yellow onion, thinly sliced

1 small head cabbage, shredded

½ batch Barbecue Sauce (page 16)

6 scallions, thinly sliced

Calories: 470
Fat: 30g
Protein: 38g
Fiber: 2.5g
Net Carbs: 5g

We like to use a combination of green and purple cabbage, but that's just for the looks of the dish, not flavor.

1 PLACE the corned beef in a large pot and fill with water halfway to the top. Add the pickling spices that come with the corned beef, if desired.

2 PLACE the pot over high heat and bring up to a boil. Reduce heat to a simmer and let cook 3 hours, or until meat is fork-tender.

3 ONCE the meat has been simmering 2½ hours, start the Braised Barbecue cabbage by sautéing the butter and onion in a large skillet over medium-high heat.

4 ONCE the onions begin to caramelize, add the cabbage and Barbecue Sauce. Stir until the cabbage has cooked down enough to get coated in the sauce. Reduce heat to a simmer and let braise 20 minutes, stirring occasionally.

5 WHEN the meat is finished cooking, remove from water and let rest 10 minutes before slicing.

6 STIR scallions into the braised cabbage just before serving under the sliced corned beef.

HELPFUL TIPS

Placing the pickling spice into a metal tea ball or a tied satchel of cheesecloth will keep it from sticking to the meat as it cooks. Personally, I don't mind the spices on the meat.

PREP TIME	COOK TIME	SERVES
40 min	50 min	12

LOW-CARB LASAGNA
WITH ZUCCHINI "NOODLES"

Lasagna with only meat and cheese has always been one of my most popular recipes, yet amazingly, I've never made it with zucchini in place of the noodles until this year. I was definitely missing out!

SHOPPING LIST

4 large zucchini, thinly sliced

1 tablespoon olive oil

2 pounds ground beef

2 cups diced celery

½ cup diced red onion

1 (15-ounce can) tomato sauce

1 teaspoon minced garlic

1 teaspoon garlic powder

½ teaspoon each, salt and pepper

CHEESE FILLING

15 ounces ricotta cheese

4 cups shredded mozzarella cheese, divided

½ cup grated Parmesan cheese

1 large egg

½ teaspoon minced garlic

2 teaspoons Italian seasoning

1 teaspoon garlic powder

¼ teaspoon pepper

Calories: 355
Fat: 18g
Protein: 41g
Fiber: 2g
Net Carbs: 6g

1 FOR best results, sprinkle sliced zucchini with a light amount of salt, and place in a colander for 20 minutes to drain excess liquid that the salt will pull out. Pat dry with paper towels.

2 PREHEAT oven to 350°. Add the olive oil, ground beef, celery, and onion to a large skillet over medium-high heat and sauté until beef has browned. Drain excess liquid.

3 ADD the tomato sauce, garlic, garlic powder, salt, and pepper to the skillet and let simmer 2 minutes. Remove from heat.

4 FOLD together all Cheese Filling ingredients, using only half the mozzarella.

5 PLACE a single layer of ⅓ the sliced zucchini at the bottom of a deep 13x9-inch baking dish. Top with all of the meat mixture. Top that with another layer of the zucchini, followed by all of the cheese mixture. Make another layer of zucchini before topping all with the remaining mozzarella cheese.

6 BAKE 50 minutes, or until the top is golden brown and bubbly. Let cool 10 minutes before slicing to serve.

POT ROAST AU JUS
Chuck Roast with Onion Pan Gravy

This pot roast is baked in a thin and savory au jus packed with a flavor very reminiscent of French onion soup. For best results, you've got to use a chuck roast—they cook faster and cook up tender.

SHOPPING LIST

1 boneless chuck roast (about 4 pounds)

Salt and pepper

¼ teaspoon garlic powder

2 tablespoons vegetable oil

1 yellow onion, large chopped

2 teaspoons minced garlic

3 cups beef stock

2 large bay leaves

2 teaspoons Worcestershire sauce

1 teaspoon dried thyme

1 teaspoon onion powder

½ teaspoon pepper

Calories: 410
Fat: 17g
Protein: 65g
Fiber: 0g
Net Carbs: 3g

1 PREHEAT oven to 325°. Generously season the chuck roast with salt and pepper, then sprinkle with garlic powder.

2 HEAT the vegetable oil in a large skillet or Dutch oven over high heat. Place the seasoned roast in the skillet and brown on all sides, about 4 minutes per side, adding the onion and garlic to the skillet as you brown the last side.

3 REMOVE from heat and add remaining ingredients, stirring to combine.

4 COVER and bake 2 hours, or until the meat is fork-tender. Serve pot roast drizzled with the au jus from the pan.

HELPFUL TIPS

For a creamier gravy, transfer au jus to a sauce pan and simmer rapidly, until reduced by about half. Remove from heat and stir in 6 tablespoons of butter.

Thick-sliced zucchini and yellow squash can be added in the last 40 minutes of baking for a full meal.

BRAISED SHORT RIBS

TENDER BEEF WITH RED WINE AND BACON

I've written a lot of recipes in the past decade, but amazingly I've never put my foolproof recipe for tender and perfect short ribs on paper. It's a restaurant-quality dish (I used to cook it in restaurants) that practically cooks itself.

SHOPPING LIST

3 slices bacon

1½ pounds beef short ribs

Salt and pepper

¼ cup diced red onion

2 teaspoons minced garlic

1 cup dry red wine

1½ cups beef stock

1 sprig fresh rosemary

2 tablespoons butter

Calories: 380
Fat: 22g
Protein: 38g
Fiber: 0g
Net Carbs: 3g

Additional beef stock and 1 tablespoon balsamic vinegar can be substituted for the red wine.

1 HEAT the bacon in a Dutch oven or large skillet over medium-high heat and cook until crispy. Remove bacon and set aside.

2 SEASON the short ribs with a generous amount of salt and pepper, and then add to the hot bacon grease in the skillet. Brown ribs well on all sides.

3 ADD the onion and garlic to the pan and cook 1 minute before deglazing the pan with the red wine, scraping any browned bits from the bottom of the pan.

4 ADD the beef stock and fresh rosemary, and reduce heat to a low simmer. Crumble the cooked bacon into the sauce. Cover and let cook 2 hours, or until beef is very tender.

5 REMOVE from heat, stir in butter, and season sauce with salt and pepper to taste before serving.

HELPFUL TIPS

Before stirring the butter into the sauce, taste it for robustness. If you feel the flavor could be more concentrated, simply raise the heat, and let the sauce reduce by ⅓ before stirring in butter.

GRILLED HERB CRUSTED SIRLOIN
My Top Way to Make Top Sirloin

Top sirloin is an absolutely great cut of steak, especially when it is cut thick (we call the best cuts "baseball-cut" as they are nearly round, like a baseball). Crusting a great cut of meat with my great Italian Herb Rub is a surefire recipe for, well, greatness!

SHOPPING LIST

4 (6- to 8-ounce) top sirloin steaks

¼ cup Italian Herb Rub (page 19)

Calories: 420
Fat: 21g
Protein: 53g
Fiber: 0g
Net Carbs: 0g

1 PREHEAT a grill or grill pan over high heat.

2 RUB the steaks generously on all sides with the herb rub.

3 PLACE the steaks on the grill and cook 8 minutes for medium rare, flipping halfway through. Let rest 5 minutes before serving.

HELPFUL TIPS

These can also be seared in a regular pan over high heat in the same amount of time as grilling, but broiling is not recommended for a cut as good as top sirloin.

These same cook times work for New York strips or ribeyes as well.

FOOLPROOF ROAST BEEF

Using the Two Secrets to a Perfect Roast

There are two secrets to a great roast beef. First, you've got to roast it "low and slow"—at a low temperature for an extended amount of time. Second, you use what we call a "salt cap" to literally seal all of the juices into the roast. This layer of salt may seem like it will make the meat too salty, but it scrapes right off after baking, and I assure you it is the same technique we all use in restaurants.

SHOPPING LIST

1 sirloin tip roast (about 4 pounds)

1 teaspoon minced garlic

1 tablespoon black pepper

½ cup kosher salt

Calories: 340
Fat: 18g
Protein: 41.5g
Fiber: 0g
Net Carbs: 0g

1 PLACE rack in center position and preheat oven to 210°.

2 PLACE the roast, fat side up, in a shallow roasting pan. Rub the garlic and pepper over all surfaces of the meat, and then cover completely with a heavy layer of kosher salt.

3 ROAST for 4–5 hours, until a meat thermometer stuck into the thickest part of the roast register 145° for medium rare. For medium, cook until 160°. For well done, cook until 170°.

4 LET rest for at least 10 minutes before scraping off kosher salt and discarding. Carve and serve.

HELPFUL TIPS

You can also use this method to cook other types of beef roasts, such as a prime rib roast.

I love making roast beef, as the leftovers make great deli meat when sliced thin.

CLAIRE'S STUFFED PUMPKIN
OUR FAMILY'S TRADITIONAL FALL MEAL

While growing up in Woonsocket, Rhode Island, Rachel learned to make this stuffed pumpkin from her mother Claire. Now it has become one of our family favorites, with only one minor adjustment to make it low-carb.

SHOPPING LIST

2 tablespoons olive oil

½ cup chopped onion

1½ cups chopped celery

1 pound ground pork

8 ounces ground beef

1 teaspoon salt

½ teaspoon black pepper

1½ teaspoons garlic powder

¼ cup beef stock

1½ teaspoons ground cloves

1½ teaspoons ground cinnamon

1½ teaspoons pumpkin pie spice

1 pie pumpkin (about 2–2½ pounds)

¼ cup sugar substitute

Calories: 255
Fat: 10g
Protein: 32.5g
Fiber: 3g
Net Carbs: 5g

Clean the pumpkin just as you would for Halloween!

1 PREHEAT oven to 350°. In a large sauté pan, heat the olive oil over medium-high heat. Add the onion and celery, and cook until tender. Remove the vegetables from the pan and set them aside.

2 PLACE the same pan over high heat. Add the ground pork, beef, salt, pepper, and garlic powder, and cook until the meat is thoroughly browned. Drain off the excess grease.

3 REMOVE from heat and stir the sautéed veggies, beef stock, cloves, cinnamon, and pumpkin pie spice into the cooked meat mixture.

4 REMOVE top from pumpkin and set aside. Scoop out the pulp (discard) and seeds (save for baking into a snack), and sprinkle the inside of the cleaned pumpkin with the sugar substitute.

5 FILL the pumpkin with the cooked meat mixture and replace the top. Place in a baking dish and bake for 90 minutes, or until the pumpkin is tender when stuck with a fork. Serve the filling with slices of the roasted pumpkin.

HELPFUL TIPS

The "pie pumpkin" needed for this recipe is the smaller type of pumpkin sometimes called a "sugar pumpkin." Don't worry, it isn't sugary!

BONELESS BARBECUE RIBS

COUNTRY—STYLE RIBS, BAKED TO PERFECTION

Boneless, country-style ribs are actually just a cut from the (mostly lean) pork loin, but when slow roasted, they melt in your mouth no different from any other rib. They often go on sale, and by weight go a lot farther than bone-in ribs, as you are buying 100% meat.

SHOPPING LIST

3 pounds country-style ribs

Salt and pepper

1 batch Barbecue Sauce (page 16)

Calories: 445
Fat: 26g
Protein: 44g
Fiber: 0.5g
Net Carbs: 4g

1 PREHEAT oven to 325°.

2 GENEROUSLY season ribs with salt and pepper, and place in a large baking dish.

3 COVER dish with aluminum foil, and bake 2 hours.

4 DRAIN excess liquid from the baking dish; add Barbecue Sauce, tossing pork in the sauce to coat.

5 BAKE an additional 30 minutes, uncovered, basting with the sauce halfway through.

HELPFUL TIPS

You can also finish these on the grill by skipping the last 30 minutes of baking, and tossing in ½ of the sauce before grilling 15 minutes. Top with additional sauce before serving.

Do not skimp on the salt and pepper when seasoning the ribs, as they are usually quite thick and need a good amount of seasoning.

THE PERFECT BROILED NEW YORK STRIP
WITH OR WITHOUT GORGONZOLA BUTTER

Though most busy people broil steaks, very few know the secret to that "perfect" broiled steak. It's two secrets actually; first, you have to start with the steaks at room temperature, and second, you've gotta preheat the pan under the broiler before cooking!

SHOPPING LIST

2 New York strip steaks, about 1 inch thick

2 teaspoons Worcestershire sauce

2 teaspoons vegetable oil

¼ teaspoon garlic powder

¼ teaspoon salt

¼ teaspoon pepper

Gorgonzola Butter (page 17), if desired

Calories: 405
Fat: 22.5g
Protein: 46g
Fiber: 0g
Net Carbs: 0.5g

1 PLACE steaks in a shallow dish with the Worcestershire sauce, vegetable oil, garlic powder, salt, and pepper. Toss to coat, and leave on counter 20 minutes to bring the steaks to room temperature.

2 PLACE a heavy broiler-safe skillet 6 inches from the broiler, and preheat the broiler to high with the skillet in the oven.

3 SHAKE all excess liquid off steaks and carefully place in the preheated skillet.

4 LET broil 4 minutes before flipping and broiling an additional 3 minutes for medium rare.

5 TOP with Gorgonzola Butter, if desired, and let rest 7 minutes before serving.

NOTE:

As the Gorgonzola Butter is optional, it has not been included in the nutritional information for this recipe.

This same method can be used to cook 1-inch thick ribeye steaks!

PEPPER STEAK STIR-FRY
Strips of Sirloin Steak with Sweet Bell Peppers

Takeout pepper steak sauce is usually sweetened with sugar and thickened with a huge amount of starch. My recipe keeps it simple and uses top-quality steak for top-quality results!

SHOPPING LIST

1 tablespoon vegetable oil

1¼ pounds sirloin steak, cut into strips

1 green bell pepper, sliced

1 red bell pepper, sliced

1 teaspoon minced garlic

3 tablespoons soy sauce

¼ teaspoon onion powder

¼ teaspoon black pepper

1 tablespoon sesame oil

4 scallions, sliced

Calories: 355
Fat: 16g
Protein: 44.5g
Fiber: 2g
Net Carbs: 4g

1 POUR the vegetable oil in a sauté pan or wok over high heat and bring up to a sizzle.

2 ADD the steak, bell peppers, and garlic, and sauté until steak has browned.

3 WHISK together the soy sauce, onion powder, and pepper, and pour into the sauté pan. Toss to coat steak and peppers, and sauté 1 additional minute.

4 STIR in sesame oil and scallions and remove from heat. Serve immediately.

HELPFUL TIPS

To ensure the steak is still pink in the center, you will want to make quick work of the stir-frying. It's a good idea to have all of your ingredients laid out and ready to go before cooking.

This goes great alongside my Sesame & Spice Broccoli (page 159).

PORK TENDERLOIN WITH MUSTARD GRAVY

A Must-Make Family Meal

Pork tenderloin, the most tender cut of pork (as the name implies), is a great way to make a roast for dinner in only 30 minutes! As it bakes, you can whip up this tangy mustard gravy for a restaurant-style dish made easy, almost too easy.

SHOPPING LIST

2 pork tenderloins (about 2 pounds total)

Salt and pepper

1 tablespoon vegetable oil

½ cup diced yellow onion

1 teaspoon minced garlic

1½ cups chicken stock

1 bunch fresh thyme

2 tablespoons coarse deli mustard

¼ teaspoon onion powder

½ cup heavy cream

Calories: 285
Fat: 11.5g
Protein: 41g
Fiber: 0g
Net Carbs: 1g

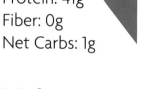

We love to serve this with grilled peaches as a garnish!

1 PREHEAT oven to 400°. Generously season the pork tenderloins with salt and pepper.

2 HEAT the vegetable oil in a large skillet over high heat. Place the seasoned tenderloins in the skillet and brown on all sides. Transfer tenderloins to a sheet pan.

3 BAKE the tenderloins for 18–25 minutes, or until a meat thermometer inserted into the thickest part reads 145°. Cover and let rest 10 minutes before slicing.

4 As the tenderloins bake, reduce the heat of the skillet to medium-high, and add the onion and garlic. Sauté for 1 minute before deglazing the pan with chicken stock, scraping any browned bits from the bottom of the pan.

5 ADD the thyme, mustard, and onion powder, and let simmer until liquid has reduced by half.

6 REMOVE from heat, stir in heavy cream, and season the sauce to taste with salt and pepper. Serve the sliced tenderloin drizzled with the mustard gravy.

HELPFUL TIPS

Before baking the tenderloins, sprinkle with a pinch of dried thyme to add some aromatics to the meat as it roasts.

BLACKENED PORK CHOPS
MY FAVORITE PORK CHOP PREPARATION

As a chef for several decades, I've made pork chops in just about every way you can imagine, but when I am cooking chops at home, I almost always default to my favorite spice blend. The Blackening Spice almost creates a crust, sealing in the pork's natural juices.

SHOPPING LIST

1 tablespoon vegetable oil

4 large pork chops, about ¾ inch thick

2 tablespoons Blackening Spice (page 18)

Calories: 285
Fat: 23g
Protein: 18g
Fiber: 0g
Net Carbs: 0g

1 TURN your overhead exhaust fan on before cooking.

2 PLACE the oil in a large skillet over high heat, and heat until almost smoking.

3 GENEROUSLY season both sides of the pork chops with the Blackening Spice before placing the chops in the skillet.

4 COOK pork chops 4 minutes on each side until well seared, and the thickest chop is cooked throughout.

HELPFUL TIPS

This can be made with any kind of pork chops, even lean and boneless pork loin chops.

The Blackening Spice will create a lot of smoke as it cooks, but that is entirely normal.

BAKED HAM WITH ORANGE GLAZE
A "Zesty" and Sweet Holiday Ham

A glazed ham is a staple around the holidays, and you don't have to give that up if you've given up sugar. This recipe makes a glaze from the sugar substitute of your choice (including the new natural substitutes!) and fresh orange zest that adds more flavor than honey ever does.

SHOPPING LIST

1 bone-in smoked ham (8–10 pounds)

GLAZE

1 teaspoon dry mustard

1 teaspoon white vinegar

¾ cup sugar substitute

2 tablespoons water

1 tablespoon grated orange zest

Calories: 210
Fat: 8g
Protein: 29g
Fiber: 0g
Net Carbs: 3g

1 PLACE oven rack in lowest position and preheat oven to 325°.

2 PLACE the ham fatty side up in a shallow baking pan, loosely cover with aluminum foil, and bake 1 hour.

3 MEANWHILE, whisk together all Glaze ingredients, and set aside until ham has baked.

4 REMOVE the baked ham from oven and use a sharp knife to make shallow cuts in a criss-crossed fashion over the fatty side of the ham. Pour the glaze over top of the cuts, and let it drip down over all edges of the ham.

5 BAKE uncovered for an additional 30 minutes. Let rest 10 minutes before carving.

HELPFUL TIPS

If you like cloves, this is also good with whole cloves stuck into the cuts in the ham before adding the glaze. Remove cloves and discard before carving.

"Scoring" the ham with a crosshatch of cuts allows the flavor of the orange zest to bake into the meat of the ham.

SAUSAGE STUFFED SPAGHETTI SQUASH
DINNER, IT'S COOKING IN THE SQUASH

We've been cooking our spaghetti squash separately from the sauces for years, but recently decided to stuff the squash before baking—the results were way better than ever before—as the squash absorbs the flavors of this Italian sausage and tomato sauce stuffing as it roasts.

SHOPPING LIST

1 medium spaghetti squash (may use 2 small)

1 pound ground Italian sausage, without casings

½ cup diced red onion

2 teaspoons minced garlic

1 green bell pepper, diced

1 cup sliced button mushrooms

1 (15-ounce) can tomato sauce

½ cup black olives, chopped

1 tablespoon Italian seasoning

2 cups grated mozzarella cheese, divided

Calories: 425
Fat: 30g
Protein: 26.5g
Fiber: 2.5g
Net Carbs: 6g

We save the squash seeds to bake like pumpkin seeds!

1 PREHEAT oven to 350°. Carefully slice the spaghetti squash in half lengthwise. Scoop the seeds from the squash, and place the cleaned squash halves in a baking dish.

2 PLACE the Italian sausage, onion, and garlic in a large skillet over medium-high heat, and sauté until sausage is browned and crumbled.

3 ADD the bell pepper and mushrooms to the skillet, and sauté an additional 3 minutes before draining any excess water or grease.

4 STIR in tomato sauce, olives, and Italian seasoning, and bring up to a simmer for 5 minutes.

5 SPRINKLE ½ of the mozzarella cheese evenly over the inside of the cleaned spaghetti squash halves, and then top with an equal amount of the cooked sausage mixture.

6 TOP the stuffed halves with the remaining mozzarella cheese, and bake 35–40 minutes. Let cool 5 minutes before serving.

HELPFUL TIPS

If you poke some holes in the spaghetti squash and microwave for just 1 minute, it will start to soften the squash to make it easier to cut in half.

Jamaican Shrimp Scampi

Scallop and Scallion
Stir-Fry

Hazelnut Crusted Tilapia

SEAFOOD

JAMAICAN SHRIMP SCAMPI
WITH RED BELL PEPPER AND HONEYDEW MELON

This recipe adds Caribbean spices to the classic shrimp scampi with delicious results. Crushed red pepper flakes add just a touch of heat that is cooled down by fresh and sweet honeydew melon.

SHOPPING LIST

4 tablespoons Scampi Compound Butter (page 17)

1 pound (16- to 20-count) peeled and deveined raw shrimp, with tails on

½ teaspoon dried thyme

¼ teaspoon ground allspice

1 pinch crushed red pepper flakes

1 tablespoon dry white wine

2 tablespoons diced red bell pepper

⅓ cup diced honeydew melon

Calories: 245
Fat: 13.5g
Protein: 26g
Fiber: 0g
Net Carbs: 3.5g

1 PLACE Scampi Compound Butter in a large sauté pan over medium-high heat.

2 ONCE the butter is sizzling, add the shrimp, thyme, allspice, and red pepper flakes, and sauté 2 minutes, stirring occasionally.

3 ADD the white wine and bell pepper, and cook until the shrimp are opaque, about 2 additional minutes.

4 REMOVE from heat and stir in honeydew melon before serving.

HELPFUL TIPS

This goes great with a modified version of my Southwestern Cauliflower Rice (page 166). Omit the cilantro, cumin, and Cheddar-Jack cheese, and add a pinch of allspice, and you've got Caribbean Cauliflower Rice!

Cantaloupe, or even kiwi, work great in place of the honeydew melon.

HAZELNUT CRUSTED TILAPIA

Flaky White Fish with a Nutty Crust

I was always taught that white fish were to be crusted with lighter colored macadamias or almonds, while darker fish (such as salmon) were to be crusted with pecans, walnuts, or hazelnuts—but I've had a real change of heart on that—because simply, it tastes great!

SHOPPING LIST

Nonstick cooking spray

2 tilapia fillets

1 ounce white wine, optional (may use water)

2 teaspoons fresh lemon juice

1 tablespoon mayonnaise

2 tablespoons butter, softened

1 teaspoon Dijon mustard

¼ teaspoon kosher salt

⅛ teaspoon black pepper

¼ cup crushed or finely chopped hazelnuts

Calories: 370
Fat: 23g
Protein: 35g
Fiber: 1g
Net Carbs: 3g

1 PREHEAT oven to 375°, and spray a baking dish with nonstick cooking spray.

2 PLACE the tilapia fillets in the baking dish, and drizzle with the wine and lemon juice.

3 ADD remaining ingredients, except the hazelnuts, to a medium bowl, and mix well to create a glaze.

4 TOP the fish with even amounts of the glaze, and then sprinkle with the crushed hazelnuts.

5 BAKE for 15 minutes, or until the fish starts to brown, and easily flakes with a fork. Serve basted in the pan juices and garnished with lemon wedges, if desired.

HELPFUL TIPS

Any white fish, such as sole or flounder, can be used in place of the tilapia.

If you prefer, walnuts or pecans can easily be substituted for the hazelnuts to make this to your liking!

CLAM FRITTERS

LIKE HUSHPUPPIES, BURSTING WITH CLAMS

These fried fritters filled with baby clams are a perfected version of one of my oldest recipes, Rocky Point Clam Cakes (as I used to call them). To be honest, they were always more of a fritter than a cake, and recently I've entirely changed the way I make the dough for a far, far better low-carb dough that is a huge improvement on the original. Even after all these years, I am constantly tweaking and perfecting my recipes!

SHOPPING LIST

4 cups trans-fat-free frying oil

1 (10-ounce) can baby clams in water

1 cup Almond Flour (page 14)

½ cup milled flax seed

2 large eggs

1 tablespoon baking powder

1 teaspoon salt

½ teaspoon black pepper

¼ teaspoon garlic powder

Calories: 200
Fat: 17g
Protein: 9.5g
Fiber: 3.5g
Net Carbs: 2.5g

For even more flavor, dust the fritters with Old Bay Seasoning right after you remove them from the oil.

1 ADD the frying oil to a heavy pot, leaving at least 4 inches to the top, and place over medium-high heat, or use an electric deep fryer filled to the fill line, and preheated to 350°.

2 ADD all ingredients (including liquid from the canned clams) to a large mixing bowl, and stir until mixture reaches a thick, but smooth consistency.

3 USING a spoon, drop 5 walnut-sized spoons of the batter into the hot oil.

4 FRY the fritters in small batches of no more than 5 fritters, cooking each batch about 3 minutes, or until golden brown. Transfer to paper towels to drain excess oil.

5 REPEAT this process until all batter has been used. Serve hot.

HELPFUL TIPS

You can find canned clams near the canned tuna in any grocery store. They should be labeled "baby clams in water." Stay away from "smoked" clams, which are usually packed in oil.

TILAPIA VERACRUZ

Tilapia with a Fresh Mexican "Tomato Sauce"

This Mexican preparation of tilapia is topped with a fresh "tomato sauce" that is a whole lot like a warm pico de gallo. Green olives are the secret ingredient, bringing a briny goodness to the fresh tomatoes and delicate fish.

SHOPPING LIST

1 tablespoon olive oil

4 tilapia fillets

Salt and pepper

1 tablespoon finely diced jalapeño

2 tablespoons diced red onion

1 tomato, diced

¼ cup chopped green olives

Juice of ½ lime

1 tablespoon chopped
  fresh oregano

Calories: 190
Fat: 6.5g
Protein: 32g
Fiber: 1g
Net Carbs: 2g

1 PLACE the olive oil in a large sauté pan over medium-high heat.

2 SEASON the tilapia with salt and pepper, and add to the pan. Let sear for 3 minutes without moving the fish.

3 FLIP tilapia and let cook 2 additional minutes before removing from pan and covering.

4 ADD remaining ingredients to the pan and sauté for 2 minutes, just until the onion begins to sweat. Season to taste with salt and pepper and serve over the cooked tilapia.

HELPFUL TIPS

Any kind of seafood can be cooked Veracruz in place of the tilapia. Shrimp or scallops are especially good, but the cook time should be reduced to only 4 minutes.

Top this with diced avocado, or serve with prepared guacamole for even more flavor!

PREP TIME	COOK TIME	SERVES
15 min	4 min	4

SCALLOP AND SCALLION STIR-FRY
WITH YELLOW SQUASH, RED BELL PEPPER, AND SNOW PEAS

Not many people think of scallops when it comes to shopping for a stir-fry, but their natural sweetness perfectly complements the savory flavor of soy sauce. Plus, they cook so fast that you not only have dinner in 5 minutes, but you've ensured that the vegetables stay crisp-tender—something that isn't always easy to do in a one-pot meal.

SHOPPING LIST

2 tablespoons vegetable oil

2 teaspoons sesame oil

1 pound bay scallops

1 yellow squash, cut into 1-inch sticks

1 cup snow peas

½ red bell pepper, thinly sliced

1 small bunch scallions, ends trimmed and sliced into 1-inch lengths

1 clove garlic, crushed

2 tablespoons soy sauce

¼ teaspoon black pepper

Toasted sesame seeds, for garnish

Calories: 220
Fat: 10.5g
Protein: 22g
Fiber: 3g
Net Carbs: 6g

1 POUR the vegetable oil and sesame oil in a sauté pan or wok over medium-high heat, and bring up to a sizzle.

2 ADD the scallops, yellow squash, snow peas, and bell pepper to the pan and sauté, stirring occasionally, for 2 minutes.

3 ADD the scallions, garlic, soy sauce, and black pepper, and sauté an additional 2 minutes.

4 REMOVE from heat and serve immediately, garnished with toasted sesame seeds, if desired.

HELPFUL TIPS

Any combination of vegetables can be used in place of the yellow squash, snow peas, and red bell pepper—but the scallions are what truly makes this great!

Bay scallops are the smaller scallops and are more suited to a stir-fry where you can get a whole scallop in almost every bite.

LEMON PEPPER TILAPIA
MADE WITH REAL LEMONS, NOT THE SPICE RACK

Lemon pepper is one of the most popular "spices" around, but I've never seen the point in shaking fake lemon flavor onto food when real, fresh lemons are so inexpensive and taste so much better. For that concentrated flavor, you just have to use the zest!

SHOPPING LIST

1 tablespoon olive oil

1½ pounds tilapia fillets

Juice of 1 lemon

½ teaspoon lemon zest

1 teaspoon minced garlic

¼ teaspoon salt

½ teaspoon freshly cracked
    black pepper

Calories: 170
Fat: 5g
Protein: 32g
Fiber: 0g
Net Carbs: 0.5g

1 PREHEAT oven to 375°, and grease a sheet pan with olive oil. Place tilapia fillets on greased sheet pan.

2 ADD remaining ingredients to a small bowl, mix well, and then evenly drizzle over tilapia fillets.

3 BAKE for 15 minutes, or until fish begin to turn a light brown, and easily flake with a fork. Serve basted with the juices in the pan.

HELPFUL TIPS

For even more flavor, gently toss the fish in a bowl with the lemon pepper sauce, and marinate in the refrigerator for 10 minutes as the oven preheats.

Garnish the plate as you would most seafood dishes, with fresh lemon slices or wedges.

GRILLED SWORDFISH WITH GINGER BUTTER

Asian–Style Swordfish Steaks

Recipes like this one are the reason I always keep a few different Compound Butters in my fridge or freezer. With the butter on hand, you can have an amazing dish in only minutes.

SHOPPING LIST

4 swordfish steaks

2 tablespoons sesame oil

3 tablespoons soy sauce

1 teaspoon minced garlic

¼ teaspoon black pepper

Ginger Compound Butter (page 17)

Calories: 300
Fat: 19.5g
Protein: 28g
Fiber: 0g
Net Carbs: 1g

Note: Nutritional information includes one serving of Ginger Compound Butter.

1 PLACE swordfish steaks in a shallow dish with the sesame oil, soy sauce, garlic, and pepper. Toss to fully coat fish. Cover and let marinate at least 15 minutes.

2 PREHEAT a grill or grill pan over medium-high heat.

3 PLACE swordfish on the hot grill and cook 6–10 minutes, flipping halfway through. Grill 6 minutes for thin steaks and 10 minutes for extra thick steaks.

4 REMOVE from grill and serve topped with a pat of Ginger Compound Butter.

HELPFUL TIPS

If you'd like to try the swordfish with one of my other Compound Butters, simply marinate the fish in olive oil in place of the sesame, and lemon juice in place of the soy sauce. Add ¼ teaspoon salt to replace the salt from the soy sauce.

I like to garnish this (as I do most Asian-influenced dishes) with toasted sesame seeds.

WHITE FISH EN PAPILLOTE
Fish Baked in Parchment Packets

Baking fish in packets of parchment paper makes for not only a beautiful presentation, but ensures that the fish stays moist, even if overcooked. Simply put, this master recipe for any kind of lean white fish with any of my flavored Compound Butters is nearly impossible to mess up!

SHOPPING LIST

4 fillets white fish (see tip)

4 tablespoons any Compound Butter (page 17)

Calories: 340
Fat: 13.5g
Protein: 52g
Fiber: 0g
Net Carbs: 0.5g

1 PREHEAT oven to 350° and set out a sheet pan.

2 LAY out 4 squares of parchment paper and place a fish fillet atop each.

3 TOP each fillet with 1 tablespoon of Compound Butter.

4 FOLD all sides of the parchment papers up and crimp the edges to seal into packets.

5 PLACE packets on the sheet pan and bake 15 minutes. Serve right inside the packet, if desired.

HELPFUL TIPS

Any kind of lean white fish works great in this. Try cod, tilapia, sole, grouper, haddock, or halibut. Nutritional information is provided for cod (8 ounces) with Dill Compound Butter, though most white fish and the different varieties of Compound Butter are nearly identical in nutritional values.

Aluminum foil can be used in place of parchment paper, though it doesn't make as nice a presentation.

ROASTED ROSEMARY SALMON

A Simple "Master" Recipe for Roasted Salmon

This simple recipe for salmon can be used to roast any fatty (good fats!) fish with any herb of your choosing. I chose rosemary, as it really adds a wonderful depth while roasting, but thyme or tarragon (which has an almost licorice taste) are also great choices.

SHOPPING LIST

Nonstick cooking spray

2 pounds salmon

1 tablespoon chopped fresh rosemary

1 tablespoon olive oil

2 teaspoons lemon juice

1 teaspoon minced garlic

¼ teaspoon salt

⅛ teaspoon pepper

Calories: 335
Fat: 17.5g
Protein: 44g
Fiber: 0g
Net Carbs: 0.5g

1 PREHEAT oven to 425°, and generously spray a sheet pan with nonstick cooking spray. Place salmon on greased sheet pan.

2 ADD remaining ingredients to a small bowl, mix well, and then evenly spread over salmon.

3 BAKE for 13 minutes, or until salmon is tender and flaky.

HELPFUL TIPS

Lining the sheet pan with parchment paper will ensure the salmon doesn't stick, while also making for easier cleanup.

Skip the chopping, and top the salmon with whole sprigs of rosemary for easier prep. Simply remove before serving.

MEDITERRANEAN SHRIMP SAUTÉ

SHRIMP WITH TOMATOES, KALAMATA OLIVES, AND FETA CHEESE

This dish of shrimp in a light tomato sauce full of Mediterranean flavors is a trip to Greece in a bowl. Cooked in less than ten minutes, you'd swear that it took hours to develop these flavors!

SHOPPING LIST

1 tablespoon olive oil

1½ pounds large peeled and deveined raw shrimp, with tails on

2 teaspoons minced garlic

1 (15-ounce) can diced tomatoes

¼ cup kalamata olives

¼ cup dry white wine

1 tablespoon chopped fresh Italian parsley

½ teaspoon dried oregano

¼ teaspoon salt

¼ teaspoon pepper

1 pinch crushed red pepper flakes

⅓ cup crumbled feta cheese

Calories: 310
Fat: 10g
Protein: 41.5g
Fiber: 1.5g
Net Carbs: 5g

1 PLACE olive oil in a large sauté pan over medium-high heat.

2 ONCE the oil is hot, add the shrimp and garlic, and sauté 2 minutes, stirring occasionally.

3 ADD remaining ingredients, except feta cheese, and bring the liquid up to a simmer. Reduce heat and let simmer 3 minutes, or until shrimp are opaque.

4 SERVE topped with crumbled feta cheese and additional chopped parsley, if desired.

HELPFUL TIPS

For a full meal, serve this over roasted spaghetti squash or my Summer Squash Sauté (page 155).

The wine in this recipe can be substituted with 1 tablespoon of white or red wine vinegar.

Roasted Brussels Sprouts

Bacon & Cheddar Mock Mashed Potatoes

Summer Squash Sauté

SIDES

ROASTED CAULIFLOWER
Nutty, Caramelized Nuggets of Greatness

Much like Brussels sprouts, cauliflower transforms into something incredible when you roast it. The natural sweetness (which you wouldn't even think cauliflower had) comes out, and it takes on a nutty, toasted pecan-like flavor. We use cauliflower to reinvent a lot of comfort foods—usually with the intention of masking the flavor of the cauliflower—but this recipe is the exact opposite, celebrating cauliflower for what it truly is.

SHOPPING LIST

1 head cauliflower, cut into florets

2 tablespoons olive oil

½ teaspoon salt

¼ teaspoon pepper

⅛ teaspoon garlic powder

Calories: 75
Fat: 7g
Protein: 1g
Fiber: 2g
Net Carbs: 1.5g

1 PREHEAT oven to 400°.

2 TOSS cauliflower in olive oil, salt, pepper, and garlic powder.

3 PLACE the coated cauliflower on a sheet pan in a single layer, and bake 20–25 minutes, or until it is golden brown.

HELPFUL TIPS

You should pat the cauliflower dry with paper towels after washing it—if the cauliflower is too wet, it will take longer to caramelize, and most likely overcook before it finally does.

This goes especially great alongside any meal where you would typically serve roasted potatoes.

STUFFED EGGPLANT PARMESAN

A Classic Dish, Deconstructed and Stuffed Inside Itself

Everyone loves Eggplant Parmesan, but it isn't exactly the easiest dish to make and make well. This recipe takes all of the great flavors of the classic Italian dish and stuffs them into the eggplant itself without the need to fry anything before baking.

SHOPPING LIST

2 small eggplants, or 1 large

2 tablespoons olive oil

2 teaspoons minced garlic

2 tomatoes, chopped

¼ teaspoon dry oregano

¼ teaspoon dry basil

¼ teaspoon kosher salt

¼ teaspoon black pepper

1 cup shredded mozzarella cheese

Calories: 175
Fat: 13g
Protein: 9g
Fiber: 3.5g
Net Carbs: 4.5g

Drizzle with a little extra virgin olive oil before serving for even more flavor.

1 PREHEAT oven to 350°. Slice tops off the eggplants, and discard.

2 SLICE eggplants in half lengthwise and use a spoon to scoop out the pulp in chunks as large as possible. Scoop until eggplant skins are about ½ inch thick.

3 ADD olive oil to a nonstick skillet over medium-high heat. Roughly chop the removed eggplant pulp, add to the hot pan with the garlic, and sauté for 3 minutes.

4 REMOVE pan from heat, and add the tomatoes, oregano, basil, salt, and pepper. Mix all to combine, and make the filling.

5 PLACE eggplant shells on a baking sheet, and stuff each with an even amount of the filling. Top all with the mozzarella cheese.

6 BAKE for 30 minutes, or until the eggplant skin is soft and the cheese starts to brown. Serve immediately.

HELPFUL TIPS

Try adding cooked crumbled Italian or breakfast sausage to the filling to make a hearty meal out of this recipe!

LOADED CAULIFLOWER MUFFINS
WITH BACON AND CHEDDAR

These savory muffins make a great dinner side or snack. The cauliflower adds a nice crunchy texture while Cheddar cheese, Parmesan, and bacon make them irresistible in flavor!

SHOPPING LIST

1 cup cauliflower, small chopped

Nonstick cooking spray

½ cup Almond Flour (page 14)

½ cup chopped cooked bacon or bacon bits

½ cup shredded sharp Cheddar cheese

1 cup almond milk

¼ cup grated Parmesan cheese

¼ cup milled flax seed

3 large eggs

1 tablespoon baking powder

¼ teaspoon onion powder

¼ teaspoon salt

¼ teaspoon black pepper

Calories: 160
Fat: 13.5g
Protein: 8g
Fiber: 2g
Net Carbs: 1g

1 BRING a small pot of water to a boil. Cook the chopped cauliflower in the boiling water until crisp-tender, about 3 minutes. Drain well and pat between several layers of paper towels to dry. Set aside.

2 PREHEAT oven to 375°. Grease a 12-cup muffin tin with nonstick cooking spray.

3 IN a large bowl, combine cooked cauliflower and remaining ingredients, mixing well.

4 BAKE 20–25 minutes, until the tops of the muffins begin to brown. The muffins are done when lightly browned and a toothpick inserted into the center of a muffin comes out mostly clean. Let cool 5 minutes before serving.

HELPFUL TIPS

I always like to lightly salt the water I cook vegetables in, the same as you would pasta water. This way the salt cooks into the vegetables themselves.

These muffins are great cold, too, so don't be afraid of leftovers!

CRANBERRY SAUCE TERRINE
LIKE THE CANNED STUFF, ONLY REAL

I've had cranberry sauce or "relish" in my books since the very beginning, but surprisingly, I've never attempted to make a cold, gelatin version of cranberry sauce like we used to buy in a can before we started low-carb. I know chefs, especially fresh food chefs like myself, are supposed to look down on that kind of thing—but I always loved canned cranberry sauce!

SHOPPING LIST

1 (0.25-ounce) envelope unflavored gelatin

2 tablespoons cold water

1 cup water

1 cup sugar substitute

12 ounces cranberries

Calories: 25
Fat: 0g
Protein: 1g
Fiber: 1g
Net Carbs: 3g

1 STIR the gelatin into the 2 tablespoons of cold water to "bloom." Let rest as you continue.

2 PLACE 1 cup water and sugar substitute in a sauce pot over high heat and bring to a boil.

3 ADD cranberries to the pot and bring back up to a boil before reducing heat to a simmer. Let simmer 10 minutes, stirring occasionally.

4 REMOVE from heat and stir in bloomed gelatin. Let cool 5 minutes before transferring to a gelatin mold or baking dish. Refrigerate at least 1 hour or until set.

HELPFUL TIPS

You can also pour the Cranberry Sauce into an empty, cleaned tin can as the mold! This will make for easy slicing, just as we had our cranberry sauce growing up.

Fresh or frozen cranberries will both work in this recipe. We buy extra fresh, and freeze for year-round use.

SUMMER SQUASH SAUTÉ

Squash, Zucchini, and Cherry Tomatoes Served Up Fast

This "master" recipe for sautéed vegetables is one of my favorites to prepare in the summer when yellow squash and zucchini are always on sale. That said, you can adapt this exact same technique to sauté any vegetable quick and easy!

SHOPPING LIST

1 tablespoon olive oil

½ cup sliced red onion

2 yellow squash, sliced

2 zucchini, sliced

2 teaspoons minced garlic

¼ teaspoon salt

⅛ teaspoon pepper

⅓ cup grape tomatoes, halved

2 tablespoons thinly sliced basil

Calories: 85
Fat: 4g
Protein: 2g
Fiber: 3g
Net Carbs: 5g

1 HEAT the olive oil in a skillet over medium-high heat.

2 ADD the onion, yellow squash, zucchini, garlic, salt, and pepper, and cook, stirring occasionally, until vegetables are crisp-tender, about 3 minutes.

3 ADD the cherry tomatoes and basil, and continue to sauté an additional minute before serving.

HELPFUL TIPS

Slice the yellow squash and zucchini on a "bias" (a slight angle that makes ovals, rather than perfectly circular discs) for the best presentation.

Garnish with shredded or shaved Parmesan cheese to make this even better!

SWEET POTATO CAKES
A Sweet and Savory Sidekick

These Sweet Potato Cakes (or "pancakes" or "latkes") are a more versatile side dish than you may think. Try serving them alongside steak, turkey, pork, or you can even top them with pico de gallo and sour cream to serve alongside southwestern dishes.

SHOPPING LIST

2 large eggs

½ teaspoon baking powder

¼ teaspoon garlic powder

½ teaspoon salt

¼ teaspoon black pepper

¼ cup milled flax seed

1 cup grated sweet potato

¼ cup grated Parmesan cheese

1 tablespoon minced red onion

2 tablespoons olive oil, divided

Calories: 195
Fat: 13g
Protein: 9g
Fiber: 4g
Net Carbs: 8.5g

1 WHISK together the eggs, baking powder, garlic powder, salt, and pepper in a large mixing bowl.

2 FOLD the flax seed, sweet potato, Parmesan cheese, and onion into the egg mixture, folding until thoroughly combined.

3 COAT a nonstick skillet with a teaspoon of the olive oil. Working in batches, drop heaping tablespoons of the potato cake batter into the pan (as many as will fit) and cook for 2 minutes on each side until golden brown.

4 REPEAT the process using more oil, as needed, until all of the batter has been used. Serve hot.

HELPFUL TIPS

To grate the sweet potatoes, simply use the largest holes on your cheese grater.

For something with even lower carbs, you can substitute zucchini for the sweet potatoes.

ITALIAN EGGPLANT FRIES

DIPPABLE EGGPLANT PARMESAN

These Eggplant Fries are breaded and fried much like Eggplant Parmesan, but made for dipping! While you wouldn't confuse them for French fries, they are FAR lower in carbs, and a unique and fun way to eat your veggies.

SHOPPING LIST

4 cups trans-fat-free frying oil

3 large eggs

¼ cup water

1½ cups Almond Flour (page 14)

½ cup grated Parmesan cheese

1 teaspoon Italian seasoning

½ teaspoon salt

½ teaspoon black pepper

½ teaspoon garlic powder

2 medium eggplants

Calories: 215
Fat: 19g
Protein: 8.5g
Fiber: 3g
Net Carbs: 2g

Try these fries with warmed marinara sauce for dipping!

1 ADD the frying oil to a heavy pot, leaving at least 4 inches to the top, and place over medium-high heat, or use an electric deep fryer filled to the fill line, and preheated to 350°.

2 WHISK the eggs and water together in a medium bowl. In a larger bowl, combine the Almond Flour, Parmesan, Italian seasoning, salt, black pepper, and garlic powder to create a breading.

3 CUT the ends off the eggplants, and slice them lengthwise into ½-inch thick slices. Cut those slices into ½-inch thick sticks about the size of French fries.

4 TOSS the eggplant sticks into the breading, then the eggs, and then back into the breading, coating well.

5 PAT off any excess breading and carefully place the breaded eggplant into the hot oil. Fry until golden brown and crisp, 1–2 minutes. Repeat in batches until all eggplant is fried. Drain on paper towels and serve immediately.

HELPFUL TIPS

Be careful when frying these, as eggplant has a lot of water content which may make the oil splatter.

PREP TIME	COOK TIME	SERVES
10 min	15 min	6

SESAME & SPICE BROCCOLI

Asian–Style Broccoli with a Serious Sriracha Kick

Sriracha has exploded in popularity recently, and for good reason—it is an undeniably great hot sauce that packs not only heat, but real flavor. That flavor goes great in this Asian broccoli side dish that is roasted (for even more flavor), not stir-fried.

SHOPPING LIST

Nonstick cooking spray

1 pound broccoli spears (see tip)

2 tablespoons sriracha sauce

2 tablespoons olive oil

1 tablespoon soy sauce

1 teaspoon sesame oil

1 teaspoon sugar substitute, optional

½ teaspoon minced garlic

¼ teaspoon black pepper

Calories: 70
Fat: 5g
Protein: 2.5g
Fiber: 2g
Net Carbs: 3g

1 PREHEAT oven to 375°.

2 SPRAY an 8x8-inch baking dish with nonstick cooking spray, and place the broccoli inside.

3 WHISK together remaining ingredients to create a sauce.

4 POUR the sauce over the broccoli spears inside the baking dish, and bake for 10–15 minutes, or until broccoli starts to brown. Serve immediately.

HELPFUL TIPS

You can make this recipe with either fresh or frozen broccoli spears or florets (but I prefer the heartier spears). Fresh broccoli will have more of a crunch.

You can find sriracha in either the hot sauce or Asian foods section of the grocery store.

ASPARAGUS AND GORGONZOLA GRATIN
A Classic Steakhouse Side Dish

This side dish of asparagus baked with creamy Gorgonzola cheese is a simple but impressive way to complete a meal. I consider this something of a "master" recipe, as you could easily substitute any vegetable and any type of cheese to make the gratin of your choice.

SHOPPING LIST

1–1¼ pounds asparagus

½ cup crumbled Gorgonzola cheese

2 tablespoons butter, melted

1 teaspoon minced garlic

¼ teaspoon salt

⅛ teaspoon pepper

Calories: 145
Fat: 11g
Protein: 7.5g
Fiber: 3g
Net Carbs: 2.5g

For a true gratin with "breadcrumbs," sprinkle about 2 tablespoons of Almond Flour (page 14) over the Gorgonzola cheese before baking.

1 PREHEAT oven to 400°, and bring a pot of water to a boil over high heat.

2 TRIM 1–2 inches of the stalks off of the asparagus and drop into the boiling water, blanching for just 2 minutes for pencil-thin asparagus or 3–4 minutes for thicker asparagus.

3 TRANSFER blanched asparagus to a shallow baking dish, and top with the crumbled Gorgonzola cheese.

4 IN a small mixing bowl, combine melted butter, garlic, salt, and pepper, and then pour evenly over all in the baking dish.

5 BAKE 10 minutes, just until the Gorgonzola cheese has melted and begun to brown. Serve immediately.

HELPFUL TIPS

To keep the asparagus nice and green, transfer to a bowl of ice water after blanching in step 2. Drain well before adding to the baking dish.

JALAPEÑO & CHEDDAR CORN-LESS CORNBREAD
CORNBREAD WITHOUT ANY PROCESSED CORN? YOU BET!

Almond flour perfectly mimics cornmeal (without the carbs) in this twist on your classic sweet and savory cornbread. I mix in diced jalapeño and Cheddar cheese to add more color, flavor, and spice, though you can substitute red bell pepper in place of jalapeño if you want to play it "cool."

SHOPPING LIST

Nonstick cooking spray

1 cup Almond Flour (page 14)

½ cup sugar substitute

1½ teaspoons baking powder

3 large eggs

½ cup heavy cream

1 teaspoon vanilla extract

½ cup shredded Cheddar cheese

2 tablespoons finely diced jalapeño

Calories: 200
Fat: 17g
Protein: 9g
Fiber: 2g
Net Carbs: 2g

1 PREHEAT oven to 375°, and spray an 8-inch oven-proof skillet with nonstick cooking spray.

2 IN a large bowl, whisk the Almond Flour, sugar substitute, and baking powder. Add the eggs, heavy cream, and vanilla, and continue to whisk until completely blended.

3 FOLD in Cheddar cheese and jalapeño, and then pour the batter into the prepared skillet.

4 BAKE for 25 minutes, or until the top starts to brown. The bread is done when lightly browned and a toothpick inserted into the center comes out mostly clean. Let cool at least 5 minutes before serving.

HELPFUL TIPS

To serve the bread, use a knife or spatula to separate the edges from the skillet. Place a large serving plate over the top of the skillet and flip upside down to release.

A 6-cup muffin tin can be used in place of the skillet for baking 6 individual portions.

SIMPLY SPAGHETTI SQUASH
Nature's Alternative to Pasta

Spaghetti squash is THE low-carb alternative to pasta and, best of all, you'll have no doubt that it is 100% natural! There's no question that you will run into a "saucy" dish that truly needs something to serve underneath it, and that's where spaghetti squash will come to the rescue.

SHOPPING LIST

1 spaghetti squash

Calories: 30
Fat: 0g
Protein: 0.5g
Fiber: 1.5g
Net Carbs: 5g

HELPFUL TIPS

If you are not going to serve the squash immediately, run each half under cold water to cool down and stop the cooking process. This will help keep the squash strands "al dente." Simply heat back up in the sauce you are serving the squash with, or microwave the squash strands for 30 seconds when ready to serve.

1 USING a sharp, heavy knife, cut the spaghetti squash in half lengthwise.

2 USING a spoon, scrape out seeds and fibrous pulp around the seeds. Discard pulp and save seeds to bake as a snack, if desired.

3 PIERCE the rind of both halves of the squash in several places with the tip of a sharp knife to help vent the heat as it cooks.

4 COOK according to one of the methods below, then let cool 5 minutes before using a fork to scrape out the strands of the cooked squash (separating the strands as you scrape).

MICROWAVE: Place halves cut side down on a large plate, and microwave on HIGH for 6–8 minutes, just until rind is tender when pierced with a fork.

OVEN: Place halves, cut side down, on a sheet pan, and bake at 375° for 35 minutes, or until rind is tender when pierced with a fork.

STOVE: Place halves in boiling water and boil 20–25 minutes, or until rind is tender when pierced with a fork.

Bake the seeds tossed in oil and salt in a 300° oven for 15–20 minutes to make a quick snack!

ROASTED BRUSSELS SPROUTS
A Warm "Salad" with Balsamic Vinegar and Red Onion

I've been making roasted Brussels sprouts for some time, but once I realized that their natural sweetness is made even better when drizzling with balsamic vinegar, I got the idea for this warm salad that combines roasted Brussels sprouts with pickled red onions.

SHOPPING LIST

1 pound Brussels sprouts

1 tablespoon olive oil

¼ teaspoon salt

⅛ teaspoon pepper

⅓ cup very thinly sliced red onion

3 tablespoons balsamic vinegar

Calories: 85
Fat: 4g
Protein: 4g
Fiber: 5g
Net Carbs: 5.5g

This can also be chilled to serve as a cold potluck salad.

1 PREHEAT oven to 425°.

2 SLICE Brussels sprouts in half lengthwise, and toss in olive oil, salt, and pepper.

3 PLACE the coated Brussels sprouts on a sheet pan in a single layer, and bake 15–20 minutes, shaking the pan halfway through. Sprouts are done when the outer leaves are very browned, and centers are tender.

4 WHILE the sprouts are cooking, toss onions in balsamic vinegar to allow them to pickle.

5 TOSS cooked sprouts with the pickled onions (with vinegar) before serving warm.

HELPFUL TIPS

The onions and roasted Brussels sprouts should release a lot of natural sweetness, but if the salad is too acidic for your liking, simply add a tablespoon of olive oil and a pinch of sugar substitute to cool things down.

SOUTHWESTERN CAULIFLOWER RICE

Tons of Flavor and Color, Without the Carbs

Grating cauliflower with a cheese grater makes it into the exact consistency of rice, and because cauliflower loves to absorb flavors, it wonderfully takes on all of the southwestern flavors in this recipe.

SHOPPING LIST

1 large head cauliflower

1 tablespoon butter

1 tablespoon olive oil

¼ cup diced yellow onion

¼ cup diced red bell pepper

¼ cup diced green bell pepper

½ teaspoon minced garlic

2 cups chicken broth

1 tablespoon chopped
   fresh cilantro

2 bay leaves

1 teaspoon cumin

1 teaspoon chili powder

½ teaspoon salt

¼ teaspoon black pepper

½ cup shredded Cheddar-Jack
   cheese, optional

Calories: 75
Fat: 5.5g
Protein: 3g
Fiber: 1.5g
Net Carbs: 2g

1 CUT the head of cauliflower into 4 large pieces. Grate each piece as you would cheese, using the largest holes of a cheese grater.

2 HEAT the butter and oil in a very large skillet over medium-high heat. Add the onion, bell peppers, garlic, and grated cauliflower, and sauté for 2 minutes while gently folding, being careful not to break up the cauliflower.

3 ADD the chicken stock and seasonings, and simmer for 8 minutes, stirring occasionally.

4 DRAIN any excess liquid and top with the Cheddar-Jack cheese, if desired, before serving hot.

HELPFUL TIPS

Pay close attention as the cauliflower simmers, as you want it tender, but not mushy.

A food processor with a grating blade can make quick work of grating the cauliflower in the first step.

PIZZA-STYLE ZUCCHINI
A Kid-Friendly Vegetable Side Dish

With whole halves of zucchini topped with pizza sauce and mozzarella cheese, these are just like French bread pizzas—without the high-carb bread! You can even dice some of your favorite toppings, and add them to make these to your liking.

SHOPPING LIST

Nonstick cooking spray

2 large zucchini, ends trimmed and cut in half lengthwise

Salt and pepper

Garlic powder

½ cup prepared pizza sauce

1 cup shredded mozzarella cheese

¼ teaspoon dry oregano

1 teaspoon olive oil

Calories: 110
Fat: 7g
Protein: 9g
Fiber: 1.5g
Net Carbs: 4g

1 PREHEAT oven to 350° and spray a sheet pan with nonstick cooking spray.

2 LAY the zucchini cut side up and side by side in the center of the greased sheet pan, and generously season with salt, pepper, and garlic powder.

3 SPOON pizza sauce evenly over the zucchini, top each with equal amounts of mozzarella cheese, and then sprinkle with oregano and drizzle with olive oil.

4 BAKE for 12 minutes, or until the cheese begins to brown and bubble. Serve hot.

HELPFUL TIPS

It's perfectly fine to purchase pre-made bottled pizza sauce. There will always be natural sugars from the tomatoes, just be sure there are no added sugars in the ingredients.

You can also try this recipe with yellow squash or eggplant in place of the zucchini!

BACON & CHEDDAR MOCK MASHED POTATOES
My Famous Cauliflower Purée Made Even Better

Cauliflower purée is everywhere now, even served alongside entrées in restaurants that aren't catering to the low-carb crowd. I wrote my first recipe for "Mock" Mashed Potatoes using cauliflower a decade ago, and have only perfected it over the years. Nothing is more "perfect" than adding cheese and bacon, but you can also omit those ingredients to make my classic version.

SHOPPING LIST

1 medium head cauliflower

1 tablespoon cream cheese, softened

¼ cup grated Parmesan cheese

¼ teaspoon minced fresh garlic

¼ teaspoon chicken base (may use 1 bouillon cube, crushed, or ½ teaspoon chicken granules)

⅛ teaspoon black pepper

¼ cup shredded Cheddar cheese

4 strips cooked bacon, cut into small pieces

3 tablespoons butter, if desired

½ teaspoon chopped chives, for garnish

Calories: 170
Fat: 12
Protein: 11.5g
Fiber: 2g
Net Carbs: 2g

1 BRING a large pot of water to a boil over high heat.

2 CLEAN and cut cauliflower into small pieces. Add to the pot and boil for 6 minutes, or until well done.

3 DRAIN well, but do not let cool. Pat the cooked cauliflower between several layers of paper towels, or place cauliflower in a colander and use a heavy bowl to press the excess water out.

4 USING a food processor, pulse the hot cauliflower with the cream cheese, Parmesan, garlic, chicken base, and pepper, until almost smooth.

5 STIR in Cheddar cheese and bacon bits. Serve hot, topped with butter and chives, if desired.

HELPFUL TIPS

If the cauliflower purée cools before stirring in the cheese, simply reheat in the microwave for 1 minute.

In a pinch, we've actually had great success making this with a large bag of frozen cauliflower florets!

Blackberry & Mozzarella
Skewers

Peargaritas

Rosemary Flax Crackers

SNACKS

BLACKBERRY & MOZZARELLA SKEWERS
with Basil and Balsamic Vinegar

This is an extremely simple, yet classy appetizer that combines flavors that you didn't even know could work together! The creamy mozzarella cheese is the perfect complement to the acidity of fresh blackberries, and basil adds just the right amount of spice.

SHOPPING LIST

Bamboo skewers

12 miniature balls fresh mozzarella

12 small basil leaves

12 large blackberries

1 tablespoon balsamic vinegar

Calories: 65
Fat: 4g
Protein: 5g
Fiber: 0.5g
Net Carbs: 1.5g

1 THREAD each of the 6 skewers from bottom to top with a mozzarella ball, basil leaf, and blackberry, and repeat so there are 2 of each item on each skewer.

2 SERVE cold, drizzled with a small amount of balsamic vinegar.

HELPFUL TIPS

You can also prepare this as an antipasto-style salad by tossing all ingredients together in a bowl.

Believe it or not, a light sprinkling of fresh-cracked black pepper goes amazingly well on these!

ROADSIDE BOILED PEANUTS
THE CAVIAR OF THE SOUTH

Stopping for boiled peanuts is a rite of passage for anyone traveling the highways of the South, but few people know how easy and inexpensive it is to prepare them for yourself. While many traditional recipes are nothing more than peanuts in salted water, I like to make my boiled peanuts with a little bit of a Cajun kick, and add beef stock for a meatier flavor.

SHOPPING LIST

2 pounds raw peanuts in shell

Water, to cover

4 cups beef stock

¼ cup kosher salt

2 teaspoons crushed red pepper

2 teaspoons onion powder

1 teaspoon garlic powder

1 teaspoon chili powder

1 teaspoon pepper

1 bay leaf

Calories: 140
Fat: 11g
Protein: 6g
Fiber: 1.5g
Net Carbs: 3g

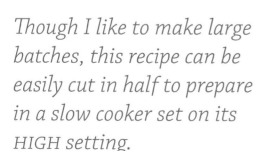

Though I like to make large batches, this recipe can be easily cut in half to prepare in a slow cooker set on its HIGH setting.

1 RINSE the peanuts thoroughly before adding to a large stock pot. For best results, cover with water and let sit for 24 hours to rehydrate (see tip) before proceeding.

2 DRAIN the soaked peanuts, and add beef stock before filling the pot with just enough water to cover the peanuts.

3 STIR in remaining ingredients, and bring to a rolling boil over high heat. Cover and reduce heat to a simmer.

4 LET simmer 4–6 hours, or until peanuts are tender. Notes: The liquid in the pot will evaporate as the peanuts simmer, so be sure to add additional water whenever necessary. Leftover boiled peanuts should be refrigerated.

HELPFUL TIPS

Raw peanuts are usually sold in the produce section of the grocery store. Unrefrigerated raw peanuts are dehydrated and require soaking or a longer cooking process (about 10 hours unsoaked). For a very short season, some stores may sell what are known as "green peanuts" in the refrigerated case. These are fresh and soft-shelled peanuts that don't require any soaking and only need to be simmered for 2–3 hours.

REAL CHEDDAR CHEESE CRISPS
A Unique Alternative to Processed Crackers

These cheese crisps are about as far from processed as a cheese "cracker" can possibly get, because they are actually made entirely of cheese! This technique is a great one to know, and can be used to make crisps out of any type of hard cheese. We like to eat these Cheddar ones as a snack, but if you substitute shredded Parmesan, you can make beautiful Parmesan crisps to garnish salads or Italian entrées.

SHOPPING LIST

2 ounces finely shredded
   Cheddar cheese

Paprika

Salt

Calories: 60
Fat: 4.5g
Protein: 4g
Fiber: 0g
Net Carbs: 0g

1 PREHEAT oven to 400°, and line a sheet pan with parchment paper. A silicone baking mat can also be used for perfect results.

2 PLACE 1 teaspoon stacks of the shredded Cheddar at least 1 inch apart on the parchment paper-lined sheet pan.

3 LIGHTLY sprinkle each stack with paprika and salt.

4 BAKE until well browned and crispy, only 7–8 minutes. Cool completely before serving.

HELPFUL TIPS

Don't be too afraid of overcooking these, as undercooking will leave them soggy. You should see the edges very visibly browning when they are ready.

Rotate the baking sheet halfway through for more even cooking.

CHEDDAR JALAPEÑO CRACKERS
WITH REAL WHITE CHEDDAR AND FRESH JALAPEÑO

Crackers are one of the things you miss the most on low-carb, but I always say that you don't have to do without. These savory white Cheddar crackers pack the spice of real jalapeños—something you'd never find in a store-bought cracker! Makes 30 crackers.

SHOPPING LIST

1 cup Almond Flour (page 14), made from blanched almonds

½ cup milled flax seed

½ teaspoon kosher salt

⅛ teaspoon baking powder

2 large eggs

4 ounces grated sharp white Cheddar cheese

1 tablespoon seeded and minced jalapeño pepper

¼ teaspoon chili powder

Calories: 140
Fat: 11.5g
Protein: 7g
Fiber: 3g
Net Carbs: 1.5g

Try dipping these in a fresh salsa!

1 ADD the Almond Flour, flax seed, salt, and baking powder to a food processor, and pulse until mixed.

2 ADD the remaining ingredients and pulse until a sticky dough-like mixture is formed.

3 PLACE the dough mixture on a 12-inch length of plastic wrap, and roll up like a burrito that is about 10 inches long. Twist the ends of the plastic wrap to seal. Refrigerate for at least 1 hour, until firm.

4 PREHEAT oven to 400° and line 2 sheet pans with parchment paper. Unwrap the chilled dough. The dough will be very sticky, so be sure to use a thin, sharp knife, and work quickly as you slice the dough into about 30 thin slices. Place the slices ½ inch apart on the prepared baking sheets and press down to flatten.

5 FOR best flavor, sprinkle the crackers with salt. Bake for 12–15 minutes, until they start to brown. Cool and serve.

HELPFUL TIPS

Any type of hard cheese can be used in place of the white Cheddar, but sharper cheeses are best.

ROSEMARY FLAX CRACKERS

Crunchy Crackers with the Flavor of Focaccia Bread

I'm a big fan of Italian focaccia bread, and these crackers remind me of just that. Serve them with Italian cheeses and cured salami for the perfect antipasti platter! Makes 30 crackers.

SHOPPING LIST

Nonstick cooking spray

1 cup milled flax seed

½ cup grated Parmesan cheese

2 large eggs

1½ teaspoons stemmed and finely chopped fresh rosemary

⅛ teaspoon onion powder

Salt

Calories: 85
Fat: 7g
Protein: 6g
Fiber: 3g
Net Carbs: 0.5g

Any fresh herb can be used in place of the rosemary. Oregano is especially good!

1 PREHEAT oven to 350°, line a sheet pan with parchment paper, and spray paper with nonstick cooking spray.

2 ADD all ingredients, except salt, to a bowl, and mix well to form a sticky dough.

3 PLACE the dough on the prepared sheet pan and cover with a sheet of plastic wrap. Using a heavy can or rolling pin over the plastic wrap, roll the dough out as thin and evenly as you can. Remove plastic wrap and use a knife to score the crackers into 30 squares.

4 LIGHTLY sprinkle the rolled-out dough with salt, and bake for 10 minutes, or until crackers start to brown. Flip crackers and cook an additional 5 minutes. Cool and serve.

HELPFUL TIPS

If the crackers are still a bit soft, they may not have been rolled out thin enough. Simply turn the oven down to 275° and leave crackers in until crispy. The low temperature literally dehydrates them without over-browning.

BAKED ZUCCHINI CHIPS
Great for Low-Carb Dipping

Zucchini, much like cauliflower, is perfect for reinventing our favorite comfort foods. Veggies are frequently used to make pre-packaged chips found in the grocery store, though the added starches and flavorings make them too high in carbs for a low-carb lifestyle, so making them from scratch is best.

SHOPPING LIST

3 zucchini

1 tablespoon olive oil

2 teaspoons chili powder

1 teaspoon salt

½ teaspoon garlic powder

¼ teaspoon black pepper

⅛ teaspoon cayenne pepper

Calories: 40
Fat: 2.5g
Protein: 1.5g
Fiber: 1.5g
Net Carbs: 2g

1 PREHEAT oven to 450°, and line a sheet pan with parchment paper.

2 TRIM the ends of the zucchini and slice them into ⅛-inch thick discs. Then add the zucchini slices to a mixing bowl.

3 ADD remaining ingredients to the bowl and toss to coat zucchini slices.

4 LAY the slices in a single layer on the prepared sheet pan, and bake for 20 minutes.

5 REMOVE from oven, flip each slice, and continue baking for an additional 15 minutes, or until chips begin to brown and become crispy. Serve warm.

HELPFUL TIPS

Be careful not to use too much olive oil, as it will keep the chips from crisping. If the chips become soft, you can crisp them up again by reheating in the oven for just a few minutes.

Keep a close eye while these bake, as there is a very fine line between "crispy" and "burnt."

SAVORY CHEDDAR MINUTE MUFFIN
A Quick Lunch or Perfect Barbecue Side Dish

This savory muffin that is literally made in only a minute makes a perfect and (really) quick lunch. You can even mix up the ingredients in advance and refrigerate until lunchtime. I like to top this with leftover ham for extra protein (though it packs a lot of protein on its own).

SHOPPING LIST

¼ cup milled flax seed (golden is best)

1 tablespoon Almond Flour (page 14)

1 ounce shredded Cheddar cheese

½ teaspoon baking powder

1 large egg

1 teaspoon melted butter

⅛ teaspoon onion powder

Dash of salt and pepper

Calories: 375
Fat: 30g
Protein: 20.5g
Fiber: 9g
Net Carbs: 2g

1 ADD all ingredients to a microwave-safe coffee mug, and mix with a fork, until well combined.

2 MICROWAVE for about 1 minute on HIGH, or until batter rises in cup, and a toothpick stuck into the center comes out mostly clean. Microwaves vary, but 1 minute seems to be the minimum cooking time, so start there and add a few seconds, if needed.

3 LET cool 3 minutes before serving.

HELPFUL TIPS

Adding a pinch of Old Bay Seasoning to these makes them remind me of Cheddar Bay Biscuits from a certain seafood chain.

Any cheese can be used in place of the Cheddar!

PEARGARITAS

FROZEN MARGARITAS MADE WITH FRESH PEAR AND KIWI

Living in Florida, it's always nice to take a relaxing break from writing this cookbook and kick back by the pool. These "Peargaritas" are the perfect poolside drink to cool down and rest my recipe typing fingers!

SHOPPING LIST

1 ripe pear

1 kiwi

½ cup sugar substitute

½ cup tequila

½ cup cold water

4 ice cubes

Juice of 1 lime

Calories: 105
Fat: 0g
Protein: 0g
Fiber: 1.5g
Net Carbs: 6g

1 PEEL and chop pear and kiwi. For the thickest margaritas, freeze the chopped fruit before proceeding.

2 ADD the frozen fruit and remaining ingredients to a blender, and pulse to break up large chunks of fruit and ice.

3 BLEND on high for 2 minutes until entirely smooth. Serve immediately in 4 margarita glasses, if you have them!

HELPFUL TIPS

Garnish the glasses with rock salt and a slice of lime for the best presentation. A slice of kiwi is a nice touch as well!

It should go without saying that you can make these "virgin" by omitting the tequila.

PREP TIME	COOK TIME	SERVES
10 min	0 min	3

PUMPKIN FRAPPÉ
FROZEN COFFEE MEETS PUMPKIN PIE

We are coffee fanatics and always keep extra brewed coffee in the fridge for making ice or frozen coffee drinks like this one. Just be sure to make your coffee extra strong to mix with the almond milk, pumpkin, and ice in this frozen treat. (Extra strong is the only way I know how to brew coffee.)

SHOPPING LIST

½ cup strong coffee, chilled

1 cup unsweetened almond milk

¼ cup canned pumpkin

2 teaspoons vanilla extract

¼ teaspoon pumpkin pie spice

1½ cups ice

2–3 tablespoons sugar substitute, to taste

Calories: 25
Fat: 1g
Protein: 0.5g
Fiber: 1g
Net Carbs: 2g

1 ADD all ingredients to a blender, starting out with 2 tablespoons of sugar substitute. Depending on your tastes and the strength of your coffee, you may wish to add more sugar substitute after blending.

2 BLEND until ice has been chopped fine and the drink is smooth. Taste for sweetness and add sweetener, if desired.

HELPFUL TIPS

You can also make this with instant coffee granules in place of brewed coffee. Simply add 2½ teaspoons of granules and an extra ½ cup of almond milk.

Unsweetened soy milk can be used in place of the almond milk, if desired.

"KETTLE CORN" MIXED NUTS
Sweet, Salty, and No Sugar Added

These simple, sweet and salty mixed nuts remind me of the Kettle Corn I used to get at the carnival—of course now Kettle Corn popcorn is in stores and quite popular, but I've never had any of that stuff!

SHOPPING LIST

1 tablespoon butter, melted

2 tablespoons sugar substitute, plus additional for dusting

¼ teaspoon vanilla extract

2 cups salted mixed nuts

Calories: 155
Fat: 14.5g
Protein: 4g
Fiber: 1.5g
Net Carbs: 3.5g

Start with unsalted nuts and sprinkle with butter-flavored popcorn salt in step 4 for that true microwave "kettle corn" flavor (without all of the trans-fat).

1 PREHEAT oven to 325°, and line a sheet pan with parchment paper.

2 ADD all ingredients to a mixing bowl, and toss well to evenly coat nuts with butter and sugar substitute.

3 SPREAD the coated nuts in an even layer on the sheet pan and bake 10 minutes, stirring halfway through.

4 REMOVE from oven and sprinkle lightly with additional sugar substitute before serving.

HELPFUL TIPS

These can be made with any combination of roasted or even raw nuts and seeds. Shelled pumpkin seeds are especially good! Unsalted nuts or seeds should be salted along with the sugar substitute in step 4.

Donut Holes

Old-Fashioned Peanut
Butter Cookies

Chocolate Walnut Bon Bons

Sweet Bites

BAKED MERINGUE COOKIES
Crunchy "Marshmallow" Clouds

Meringue cookies are a natural fit for a low-carb lifestyle, as they are mostly egg whites and are not made with flour. The best part is that they have the flavor of a marshmallow—and who doesn't like marshmallows? Makes 48 cookies.

SHOPPING LIST

Nonstick cooking spray

6 large egg whites

1 teaspoon vanilla extract

¼ teaspoon cream of tartar

⅓ cup sugar substitute

Calories: 10
Fat: 0g
Protein: 2g
Fiber: 0g
Net Carbs: 1g

For the best looking Meringue Cookies, use a pastry piping bag to pipe dollops onto the sheet pans.

1 PREHEAT oven to 350° and spray 2 sheet pans with nonstick cooking spray.

2 ADD the egg whites to an electric mixer and beat on high speed until frothy, about 1 minute.

3 ADD remaining ingredients and beat until soft peaks form and meringue is shiny.

4 PLACE heaping tablespoons of the whipped meringue in evenly spaced rows on the greased sheet pans, leaving about 2 inches between each spoonful. This is easiest with 2 spoons, using the second spoon to scoop the meringue out of the first spoon.

5 PLACE sheet pans in the preheated oven and immediately turn oven off. Leave cookies in the oven for at least 2 hours as the oven slowly cools down. Do not open oven door during this process! Serve at room temperature.

HELPFUL TIPS

For cookies that are guaranteed to cleanly release from the pan, simply line with parchment paper instead of using nonstick cooking spray. The trick to holding the paper in place as you spoon out the cookies is to place 4 small dabs of the meringue in between the paper and the sheet pan at each corner of the paper, almost like glue.

PEANUT BUTTER BUCKEYES

THEY'RE NUTTY AND THEY'RE LOOKING AT ME!

Buckeyes are not only an Ohio tradition, but an instant late-night or anytime dessert! There really is nothing better than peanut butter and chocolate, and you don't have to sacrifice either on a low-carb lifestyle.

SHOPPING LIST

¼ cup smooth natural peanut butter

1 tablespoon heavy cream

2 tablespoons sugar substitute

½ teaspoon vanilla extract

Toothpicks

½ batch Chocolate Ganache (page 20)

Calories: 155
Fat: 13g
Protein: 5.5g
Fiber: 1.5g
Net Carbs: 3.5g

The best natural peanut butter is the kind with oil that needs to be stirred back into the jar.

1 ADD the peanut butter, heavy cream, sugar substitute, and vanilla extract to a bowl, and mix with a fork until the mixture thickens to the point that you cannot mix it any longer, 2–3 minutes.

2 USE your hands to roll out marble-sized balls of the thickened mixture, stick a toothpick into each ball, and refrigerate on parchment paper as you make the Chocolate Ganache.

3 WHILE the ganache is still warm, pick each peanut butter ball up by the toothpick and dip in ganache, coating ¾ of the way to the top. Place back onto parchment paper.

4 REFRIGERATE for at least 1 hour to set the chocolate. Serve cold from the fridge.

HELPFUL TIPS

For even easier peanut butter bon bons, roll the peanut butter balls in an equal mixture of unsweetened cocoa powder and sugar substitute in place of using the Chocolate Ganache.

DONUT HOLES
No Sugar Added and Gluten Free

Donuts are the quintessential "forbidden" food, but I've accepted a great challenge and re-created them without the carbs! While I haven't quite figured out how to make the whole donut, these donut holes will more than curb your cravings.

SHOPPING LIST

4 cups trans-fat-free frying oil

1 cup Almond Flour (page 14)

½ cup whole milk ricotta cheese

2 large eggs, beaten

½ cup sugar substitute, plus additional for garnish

1 tablespoon baking powder

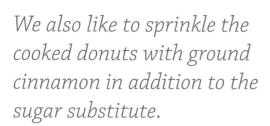

Calories: 130
Fat: 11g
Protein: 4g
Fiber: 1g
Net Carbs: 2g

We also like to sprinkle the cooked donuts with ground cinnamon in addition to the sugar substitute.

1 ADD the frying oil to a heavy pot, leaving at least 4 inches to the top, and place over medium-high heat, or use an electric deep fryer filled to the fill line and preheated to 350°.

2 ADD remaining ingredients to a large mixing bowl and stir until well combined.

3 USING a teaspoon or melon baller, quickly drop rounded spoons of the batter into the hot oil until the first few you dropped in begin to brown.

4 ONCE each is golden brown on the bottom, flip and let brown on the opposite side. Use a slotted spoon to transfer to paper towels. Immediately sprinkle with a light coating of sugar substitute.

5 REPEAT this process until all batter has been used. Serve warm.

HELPFUL TIPS

Using a pastry bag, you can stuff these donut holes with no-sugar-added jelly or my Whipped Cream (page 22).

CHEESECAKE ICE CREAM POPS

Everything is Better on a Stick

Many, many years ago, before my low-carb lifestyle, I actually had my own line of scampi butter in regional grocery stores. Because of my relationship with these stores, I was approached by a company to help them get frozen cheesecake on a stick into the same stores . . . and I did. The point of the story is, it would seem that my life has come full circle, and two decades later, I'm back to promoting cheesecake on a stick!

SHOPPING LIST

8 ounces cream cheese, softened

1½ cups half-and-half

1 teaspoon freshly squeezed lemon juice

¼ cup sugar substitute

1 teaspoon vanilla extract

Calories: 210
Fat: 20g
Protein: 4.5g
Fiber: 0g
Net Carbs: 3g

Try mixing a few chopped fresh strawberries into the mix for Strawberry Cheesecake Ice Cream Pops.

1 PLACE all of the ingredients into a food processor and blend until smooth.

2 POUR the mixture into 6 popsicle molds. You may also use ice cube trays.

3 PLACE in freezer 30 minutes, or until partially frozen. Stick popsicle sticks (or toothpicks, if using an ice cube tray) into each pop, and return to freezer. Freeze until solid.

4 REMOVE frozen pops from the molds, and serve immediately.

HELPFUL TIPS

Unsweetened almond milk can be used in place of the half-and-half to lower the fat in this recipe considerably, though natural fats aren't a bad thing on a true low-carb lifestyle. (Because your body is always burning them!)

SNICKERDOODLES

LOW—CARB COOKIES THAT ARE NOTHING TO SNICKER AT

Snickerdoodles are simple little cookies that aren't too far off from your standard butter cookies. In fact, they are nearly identical to butter cookies until they are sprinkled with cinnamon. However, I like to add a little extra cinnamon into the cookie dough itself for even more flavor.

SHOPPING LIST

2 ounces cream cheese, softened

2 tablespoons butter, softened

1 cup sugar substitute

1 large egg

1 teaspoon vanilla extract

1¼ cups Almond Flour (page 14), made from blanched almonds

½ teaspoon baking soda

½ teaspoon cinnamon

¼ teaspoon salt

CINNAMON TOPPING

2 tablespoons sugar substitute

1 teaspoon cinnamon

Calories: 150
Fat: 13g
Protein: 4.5g
Fiber: 2g
Net Carbs: 2g

You're going to want to make a double batch of these little goodies. (I know I always do!)

1 PREHEAT oven to 375°, and line a sheet pan with parchment paper.

2 USING a stand or hand-held mixer, add the cream cheese, butter, sugar substitute, egg, and vanilla extract to the mixing bowl, and beat on high until creamy and fluffy.

3 ADD in Almond Flour, baking soda, cinnamon, and salt, and mix on medium until well blended.

4 USING a teaspoon or 1 ounce ice cream scoop, drop 16 evenly spaced cookies on the prepared sheet pan, and push down slightly on each.

5 COMBINE the cinnamon topping ingredients, and sprinkle evenly over the top of each cookie.

6 BAKE for 8–10 minutes, or until they begin to brown around the edges. Let cool 10 minutes before serving.

HELPFUL TIPS

Blanched almond flour is made from slivered or "blanched" almonds without the hull. They are a must for a nice, even-looking cookie dough.

CHOCOLATE WALNUT BON BONS
WITH A CHEESECAKE CENTER

These simple bon bons have a nutty filling of walnuts and cream cheese, and taste like cheesecake with chocolate sauce! We eat these straight out of the freezer, as they can soften otherwise, but seeing as they are made with real cream cheese, they need to be kept cold regardless.

SHOPPING LIST

¼ cup chopped walnuts

2 tablespoons sugar substitute

½ teaspoon vanilla extract

4 ounces cream cheese

1 batch Chocolate Ganache
   (page 20)

Calories: 75
Fat: 7g
Protein: 2g
Fiber: 0.5g
Net Carbs: 1.5g

Any kind of nuts can be used to customize these bon bons to your liking!

1 USING a fork, mix the walnuts, sugar substitute, and vanilla into the cream cheese until well combined.

2 FORM the mixture into marble-sized balls. Line a dish that will fit into your freezer with aluminum foil, and place the balls in a single layer on the dish. Freeze for at least 20 minutes.

3 WHILE the started bon bons are chilling, prepare the Chocolate Ganache.

4 DIP the frozen walnut and cream cheese balls one at a time into the warm chocolate to coat. Place the coated bon bons back on the aluminum-foil-covered dish.

5 ONCE all bon bons have been coated, freeze for a few more minutes, just until the chocolate has hardened. Serve ice cold, as these treats DO melt in your hand.

HELPFUL TIPS

Try sticking a toothpick into the chilled cream cheese balls to more easily dip them in the warm chocolate.

PREP TIME	COOK TIME	SERVES
15 min	10 min	8

CHOCOLATE PECAN RICOTTA COOKIES
NOT YOUR COOKIE CUTTER COOKIE RECIPE

We use ricotta cheese in a lot of our baked goods as it adds moisture that most sugar substitutes lack over sugar. It also adds a great creaminess that lets us use far, far less butter in these cookies than high-carb recipes. Makes 16 cookies.

SHOPPING LIST

2 large eggs, room temperature

1 cup sugar substitute

1 tablespoon butter, softened

1 teaspoon baking powder

½ teaspoon vanilla extract

½ cup ricotta cheese

1 tablespoon unsweetened
    cocoa powder

⅛ teaspoon salt

2 cups Almond Flour (page 14)

½ cup chopped pecans

Calories: 240
Fat: 20
Protein: 9.5g
Fiber: 4g
Net Carbs: 4g

1 PLACE oven rack in the center position, and preheat oven to 350°. Line a baking sheet with parchment paper.

2 ADD all of the ingredients, except the Almond Flour and pecans, to an electric mixer, and beat on high until frothy.

3 FOLD the Almond Flour and pecans into the eggs until all is well combined.

4 USING a teaspoon or 1-ounce ice cream scoop, drop 16 evenly spaced cookies on the lined pan, and push down slightly on each.

5 BAKE for 8–10 minutes, just until they start to brown. Let cool 5 minutes before serving. Store in a covered container for up to 3 days.

HELPFUL TIPS

For the best consistency, an electric or hand mixer is recommended for making the cookie dough, though you can do it by hand in a pinch.

If you don't feel like going "nuts," just leave the pecans out, and enjoy simple delicious chocolate cookies!

ALMOND SHORTBREAD COOKIES
Low-Carb Cookies with a "Short" Shopping List

These are about as simple as low-carb cookies can get, but oftentimes the simplest recipes are the best! Flavored only with butter and the natural nuttiness of the almond flour, these may be simple, but you can't call them "vanilla."

SHOPPING LIST

2 large eggs, room temperature

1½ cups Almond Flour (page 14), made from blanched almonds

1 cup sugar substitute

1 tablespoon butter, softened

⅛ teaspoon salt

Calories: 95
Fat: 7.5g
Protein: 3.5g
Fiber: 1.5g
Net Carbs: 1.5g

Add a drop of almond extract for a stronger, amaretto flavor.

1 CRACK the eggs into a bowl and whisk until frothy.

2 ADD remaining ingredients, and mix until a very soft dough is formed.

3 PLACE the dough mixture on a 12-inch length of plastic wrap, and roll up like a burrito that is about 8 inches long. Twist the ends of the plastic wrap to seal. Refrigerate for 4 hours, or freeze for 1 hour, until firm.

4 PREHEAT oven to 375°, and line 2 sheet pans with parchment paper.

5 UNWRAP the chilled dough. The dough will be very sticky, so be sure to use a thin, sharp knife, and work quickly as you slice the dough into 24 thin slices. Place the slices 1-inch apart on the prepared baking sheets.

6 BAKE for 10 minutes, or until they start to brown. Let cool before serving. Store covered for up to 3 days.

HELPFUL TIPS

For perfectly round cookies, reshape the log of cookie dough before unwrapping and slicing.

OLD-FASHIONED PEANUT BUTTER COOKIES
Flourless, Gluten Free, and Guilt Free

These Peanut Butter Cookies may be called "Old-Fashioned" but they don't have any of the carbs, gluten, or added sugar that you'd find in the cookies of yesteryear! Makes 16 cookies.

SHOPPING LIST

1 cup smooth natural peanut butter

1 cup sugar substitute

1 large egg, slightly beaten

1 teaspoon vanilla extract

Calories: 215
Fat: 16.5g
Protein: 11g
Fiber: 2g
Net Carbs: 5g

These are almost 100% peanut butter, and that's a very good thing!

1 PREHEAT oven to 350°, and line a sheet pan with parchment paper.

2 COMBINE all ingredients in a large mixing bowl, mixing well to create the cookie dough.

3 USE a tablespoon to drop the spoonfuls of the dough 2 inches apart on the lined pan. Then use a fork to press the dough down, creating a criss-cross pattern on each cookie.

4 BAKE for 10–12 minutes, or until cookies begin to brown. Let cool for 10 minutes before serving.

HELPFUL TIPS

The criss-cross pattern often found on the top of peanut butter cookies can help people with peanut allergies easily identify it as a peanut butter cookie.

GRILLED FRUIT KEBABS

WITH CANTALOUPE, HONEYDEW, AND STRAWBERRIES

I travel the country doing "Iron Chef"-style challenges with kids at events for the Junior Leagues of America. These fruit kebabs are always a hit, and fun for the kids to help assemble. (I do the grilling!)

SHOPPING LIST

Bamboo skewers

½ cantaloupe

½ honeydew melon

2 pints strawberries, washed, dried, and hulled

Shredded coconut, for garnish

Calories: 55
Fat: 0g
Protein: 1g
Fiber: 7.5g
Net Carbs: 6g

Skewers at least 8 inches long are recommended to keep your hands away from the flames of the grill!

1 SOAK the bamboo skewers in water for 30 minutes to keep them from scorching on the grill.

2 PREHEAT a grill to medium-high, or heat an indoor grill pan on high heat.

3 TRIM rinds and remove seeds from cantaloupe and honeydew. Cut each into 2-inch chunks.

4 LEAVING about 2 inches of bamboo at the bottom of the skewer, thread a piece of cantaloupe, a whole strawberry, and then honeydew. Repeat a second time to nearly fill the skewer.

5 PLACE the kebabs on the edges of the grill (where it is less hot) and cook about 30 seconds on each of the 4 sides. Sprinkle with shredded coconut, if desired, before serving.

HELPFUL TIPS

You only want to "mark" the fruit on the grill, so do not let them cook any longer than 3 minutes total, or the fruit may fall apart.

French Vanilla
Ice Cream

Pumpkin Pecan
Streusel Pie

Stella-Style Cheesecake

Desserts

PREP TIME	COOK TIME	SERVES
30 min	1¾ hours	12

STELLA-STYLE CHEESECAKE
Our Famous New York–Style Ricotta Cheesecake

We've perfected our cheesecake recipe over the years and this is the easiest and best way that we've found to make it. It's 100% real cheesecake—without the sugar.

SHOPPING LIST

Nonstick cooking spray

24 ounces cream cheese, softened

1 cup extra fine ricotta cheese (see tips)

1½ cups sugar substitute

⅓ cup heavy cream

1 tablespoon pure vanilla extract

1 tablespoon fresh lemon juice

2 large eggs

3 large egg yolks

Calories: 270
Fat: 24g
Protein: 8.5g
Fiber: 0g
Net Carbs: 4g

HELPFUL TIPS

We usually process the ricotta cheese with a hand-blender or food processor until it is nearly as smooth as sour cream. It only takes about a minute, and helps make for the smoothest cake.

This is our most popular recipe of all time!

1 PLACE the oven rack in the center position, and preheat to 400°. Spray an 8-inch springform pan with nonstick cooking spray. Wrap the entire outside of the springform pan in aluminum foil to prevent any water from seeping into the cake.

2 MAKE a water bath so the top of the cheesecake won't split as it bakes: Pour about 1 inch hot water into a shallow roasting pan big enough to hold the cake pan, and place it on the center rack of the oven to heat.

3 WITH an electric mixer on low speed, beat the cream cheese, ricotta, and sugar substitute for about 1 minute, until well blended.

4 IN a separate bowl, whisk together the cream, vanilla, lemon juice, eggs, and yolks.

5 TURN the mixer on medium speed and slowly pour the egg mixture into the cream cheese mixture. Beat just until blended; be careful not to over-whip.

6 POUR the batter into the greased springform pan, and smooth the top with a spatula. Place the pan in the heated water bath, and bake for 15 minutes.

7 LOWER the oven temperature to 325°. Continue baking for about 1½ hours, until the top is a light golden brown and the cake is pulling away from the sides of the pan.

8 REMOVE from oven and let cool on counter for 1 hour, and then refrigerate at least 8 hours before slicing to serve.

CHOCOLATE PEANUT BUTTER CHEESECAKE SQUARES

WITH A CAKE CRUST

Chocolate Peanut Butter Cheesecake with a cakey crust and all with no sugar added and no flour? THIS is how we've maintained our weight loss!

SHOPPING LIST

CAKE CRUST

2 large eggs, beaten until frothy

1 cup Almond Flour (page 14)

¼ cup sugar substitute

1 teaspoon baking powder

FILLING

16 ounces cream cheese, softened

½ cup natural peanut butter

½ cup sugar substitute

1 tablespoon vanilla extract

4 large eggs

TOPPING

1 batch Chocolate Ganache (page 20)

½ cup chopped peanuts

Calories: 260
Fat: 22.5g
Protein: 10g
Fiber: 1.5g
Net Carbs: 4g

1 PLACE rack in the center position and pre-heat oven to 350°. Line an 8x8-inch baking dish with parchment paper.

2 ADD all of the Cake Crust ingredients to a mixing bowl and mix well. Spread the crust mixture in the prepared baking dish and bake until lightly browned, 12–15 minutes. Let cool at least 5 minutes.

3 WHILE the crust is baking, beat all Filling ingredients in an electric mixer on medium speed for 1 minute.

4 POUR the Filling over the crust and bake for 30–35 minutes, or until the center is firm and a toothpick stuck into it comes out clean. Let cool for at least 30 minutes.

5 WHILE the cake is cooling, make the Chocolate Ganache, and, working quickly, drizzle the hot ganache over the cooled cheesecake, and sprinkle the chopped peanuts over top. Refrigerate for at least 3 hours before slicing into 16 squares to serve.

HELPFUL TIPS

You can also prepare this without the Chocolate Ganache for plain Peanut Butter Cheesecake Squares.

COCONUT CAKE
WITH COCONUT BUTTERCREAM CHEESE FROSTING

This cake is an overload of coconut with coconut extract in both the cake and frosting. Real shredded coconut is sprinkled over the frosting for texture, and because, well . . . the more coconut the better!

SHOPPING LIST

Nonstick cooking spray

5 large eggs

¼ cup water

1 tablespoon coconut extract

2½ cups Almond Flour (page 14), made from blanched almonds

¾ cup sugar substitute

1 tablespoon baking powder

1 batch Buttercream Cheese Frosting (page 23), made with coconut extract

½ cup unsweetened coconut flakes

Calories: 335
Fat: 31g
Protein: 10g
Fiber: 3g
Net Carbs: 3.5g

Nutritional information for this recipe already includes the frosting.

1 PLACE oven rack in the center position, and preheat to 350°. Heavily spray an 8-inch round cake pan with nonstick cooking spray.

2 IN a large bowl, beat the eggs until frothy. Add water and coconut extract, and whisk to combine.

3 IN a medium bowl, mix the Almond Flour, sugar substitute, and baking powder. Whisk the dry ingredients into the wet ingredients until all is combined.

4 POUR the finished batter into the prepared cake pan, and bake 30–35 minutes, or until center is firm and spongy.

5 COOL on a wire rack for 30 minutes before refrigerating for at least 2 hours. Turn pan upside down and shake to release cake.

6 USING a long and thin knife, cut the cake in half horizontally to make 2 layers. Frost the bottom layer, then place the top layer over top. Frost the entire cake and finish by lightly sprinkling with unsweetened coconut flakes. Cut into 12 slices to serve.

HELPFUL TIPS

Don't forget to make the Buttercream Cheese Frosting (page 23) with coconut extract in place of the vanilla extract for the best coconut flavor in the finished cake.

PREP TIME	COOK TIME	SERVES
25 min	75 min	12

PUMPKIN PECAN STREUSEL PIE
Pumpkin Pie with a Crumbled Streusel Topping

This pumpkin pie has a crust made from chopped pecans, and a crunchy streusel topping that makes this not only low-carb, but better than most "regular" pumpkin pies!

SHOPPING LIST

CRUST

2 tablespoons butter, melted

½ cup finely chopped pecans

½ cup sugar substitute

⅛ teaspoon salt

⅛ teaspoon ground cinnamon

FILLING

1 (15-ounce) can pumpkin

¾ cup sugar substitute

1 tablespoon pumpkin pie spice

1¼ cups heavy cream

4 large eggs

STREUSEL TOPPING

3 tablespoons butter, softened

½ cup Almond Flour (page 14)

½ teaspoon ground cinnamon

¼ cup sugar substitute

Calories: 175
Fat: 16g
Protein: 4g
Fiber: 2g
Net Carbs: 3.5g

1 PREHEAT oven to 350°. Mix all Crust ingredients and press it down evenly over the bottom of a 10-inch pie pan. Bake for 5 minutes and remove from oven.

2 TURN the oven up to 425°. Whisk together all Filling ingredients and pour into the baked crust.

3 COMBINE the Streusel Topping ingredients with a fork, and crumble evenly over the top of the pie. Bake for 15 minutes at 425°.

4 REDUCE the heat to 350° and bake for an additional 50–55 minutes, or until a toothpick inserted into the center comes out mostly clean. Cool on the counter for at least 30 minutes, and then chill for at least 3 hours before serving.

HELPFUL TIPS

You just have to serve this with my Whipped Cream (page 22).

Be sure to purchase pure pumpkin and not pumpkin pie filling!

PREP TIME
15 min

COOK TIME
25 min

SERVES
8

FRENCH VANILLA ICE CREAM
Made From a Real Custard Base

True French cooking is simple at its best, and this "crème glacée" is a great example of that concept! With only four ingredients and a little attention to detail, you can create great vanilla ice cream that can also be a base for making any kind of low-carb ice cream.

SHOPPING LIST

2 cups half-and-half

5 large egg yolks

⅓ cup sugar substitute

1 teaspoon vanilla extract

Calories: 115
Fat: 10g
Protein: 3.5g
Fiber: 0g
Net Carbs: 3.5g

HELPFUL TIPS

Be careful not to let the ice cream base boil as you cook it in step 5. If it starts to get too hot, simply remove the pan from the heat, and slightly lower the stove temperature.

Try adding macadamia nuts or pecans to the mix right before freezing.

1 PREPARE an ice water bath with an insert bowl.

2 ADD 1 cup of the half-and-half to a saucepan, and heat on medium-high, until scalding hot.

3 IN a mixing bowl, beat the egg yolks with the remaining cup of half-and-half, sugar substitute, and vanilla extract.

4 TEMPER the cold egg mixture by whisking in a few tablespoons of the hot half-and-half, then whisk the tempered egg mixture into the hot pan until all is combined.

5 PLACE the pan back on the stove, and turn the heat down to medium. Cook while stirring constantly, about 20 minutes, or until the ice cream base is thick enough to coat the back of a spoon.

6 REMOVE from heat and pour the ice cream base into the insert bowl resting in the ice water bath to cool.

7 POUR the cooled custard into an ice cream maker, and follow the manufacturer's instructions to freeze the ice cream. Or for less creamy results, pour into 6 small glasses and freeze for at least 2 hours.

FUDGY FLAX BROWNIES

Made with Two Types of Chocolate and No Added Sugar

These brownies bake up dense and fudgy, exactly how you want a brownie to be. Using unsweetened baking chocolate and unsweetened cocoa powder makes the flavor intense, so only chocoholics should proceed!

SHOPPING LIST

Nonstick cooking spray

½ cup half-and-half, divided

4 ounces unsweetened baking chocolate, chopped

8 tablespoons butter, softened

2 cups sugar substitute

1 tablespoon vanilla extract

5 large eggs

¼ cup unsweetened cocoa powder

1½ cups milled flax seed

2 teaspoons baking powder

¼ cup water

Calories: 110
Fat: 10g
Protein: 3.5g
Fiber: 3g
Net Carbs: 1.5g

HELPFUL TIPS

That batter will look gritty, but that is completely normal—they will bake up perfectly.

1 PLACE oven rack in the center position, and preheat to 350°. Spray an 8x8-inch baking dish with nonstick cooking spray.

2 FILL a pot with a few inches of water, and place over medium-high heat, bringing water to a low simmer. Place a stainless steel or tempered glass bowl over the pot (above the water) to create a double boiler.

3 ADD ¼ cup of the half-and-half and all of the baking chocolate to the double boiler, and mix with a rubber spatula until chocolate is melted and creamy. Remove from double boiler and set aside.

4 USING a stand or hand-held mixer on highest speed, beat the butter until fluffy, 2–3 minutes. Add sugar substitute, vanilla extract, and remaining ¼ cup half-and-half, then continue beating as you add the eggs one at a time.

5 STOP the mixer and add the cocoa powder, flax seed, baking powder, melted chocolate mixture, and ¼ cup tap water. Mix on low for 2 minutes until all is combined.

6 SPREAD batter in the greased baking dish, and bake 35–40 minutes, or until the center is springy and a toothpick stuck into it comes out mostly clean. Let cool 30 minutes. Serve chilled for the best flavor.

Try adding walnuts or pecans to the batter.

PREP TIME	COOK TIME	SERVES
30 min	45 min	12

RASPBERRY CHEESECAKE BARS
WITH A COCONUT MACAROON CRUST

Cheesecake, coconut macaroons, and fresh raspberries all in one dessert? You bet! These cheesecake bars have real raspberries mixed right into the filling, and a crust made of shredded coconut, just as you would make macaroons.

SHOPPING LIST

Nonstick cooking spray

MACAROON CRUST

3 large egg whites

1½ teaspoons vanilla extract

½ cup sugar substitute

1 tablespoon butter, melted

½ teaspoon baking powder

1½ packed cups unsweetened shredded coconut

CHEESECAKE FILLING

16 ounces cream cheese, softened

½ cup sugar substitute

1 tablespoon vanilla extract

3 large eggs

1 cup fresh raspberries

Calories: 210
Fat: 18.5g
Protein: 6g
Fiber: 1.5g
Net Carbs: 3g

Garnish these with shredded coconut and fresh raspberries for the best presentation!

1 PREHEAT oven to 350° and spray an 8x8-inch baking dish with nonstick cooking spray.

2 ADD all Macaroon Crust ingredients to a bowl and mix well. Transfer the crust mixture into the baking dish and spread evenly. Bake until lightly browned, 12–15 minutes. Let cool.

3 As the crust is baking, add the Cheesecake Filling ingredients, including the raspberries, to an electric mixer and beat for 1 minute on medium speed, just until smooth. Do not overbeat, or the batter will be too fluffy.

4 POUR the cheesecake filling over the baked crust and bake for 30–35 minutes, or until the center is firm and a toothpick stuck into it comes out mostly clean.

5 LET cool for 30 minutes and then refrigerate for at least 3 hours before serving. Cut into 12 bars to serve.

HELPFUL TIPS

Try drizzling Chocolate Ganache (page 20), over the finished Raspberry Cheesecake Bars for even more decadence!

BUTTER PECAN POUND CAKE

This Loaf Cake is Loaded with Nutty Goodness

Pound cake is the perfect dessert to make with almond flour—as the "good" mono-unsaturated fats in the almonds make the cake moist and dense (in that good, pound cake kind of way).

SHOPPING LIST

Nonstick cooking spray

¾ cup butter, softened

6 ounces cream cheese, softened

6 large eggs, beaten until frothy

1½ teaspoons vanilla extract

1½ teaspoons lemon juice

2½ cups Almond Flour (page 14)

1¼ cups sugar substitute

2 teaspoons baking powder

½ cup chopped pecans

Calories: 250
Fat: 24g
Protein: 7g
Fiber: 2g
Net Carbs: 2.5g

You have to serve this with a big dollop of my Whipped Cream (page 22).

1 LINE a 9x5-inch loaf pan with parchment paper and spray paper with nonstick cooking spray.

2 PLACE oven rack in the center position and preheat oven to 325°.

3 WITH an electric mixer on high speed, whip together the butter and cream cheese. Add the eggs, vanilla extract, and lemon juice, and blend until smooth, about 1 minute.

4 ADD remaining ingredients, and mix by hand until all is combined and a batter is formed.

5 POUR the batter into the prepared pan and bake 1 hour, or until the top starts to brown and a toothpick stuck into the center of the cake comes out clean. Let cool at least 10 minutes before removing from pan and slicing into 8 thick pieces. Cut each piece in half again to make 16 portions.

HELPFUL TIPS

For a uniform and clean look, make the Almond Flour from blanched almonds without the brown skins. Usually the blanched raw almonds are sold as "slivered almonds" in the baking isle of your grocery store.

RED VELVET CUPCAKES

WITH BUTTERCREAM CHEESE FROSTING

As a kid, I remember having red velvet cake for special occasions, especially if we went out to a diner—which, when I was young, was actually a real treat! Mostly, I remember all those cakes rotating on pedestals inside a glass case, telling me to eat them. By making these cupcakes, rather than a layered cake, I've made it easier to prepare them on more than just those special occasions.

SHOPPING LIST

Nonstick cooking spray

5 large eggs

½ cup sour cream

1 tablespoon vanilla extract

¼ cup water

12 drops red food coloring

2½ cups Almond Flour (page 14)

¾ cup sugar substitute

3 tablespoons unsweetened cocoa powder

1 tablespoon baking powder

½ batch Buttercream Cheese Frosting (page 23)

Calories: 400
Fat: 36g
Protein: 13.5g
Fiber: 4.5g
Net Carbs: 4.5g

Garnish these with a fresh raspberry for that perfect extra touch of red.

1 PLACE oven rack in the center position and preheat to 350°. Spray 8 muffin cups with nonstick cooking spray, or line with paper liners. (You will most likely need to use a 12-muffin tin or two 6-muffin tins.)

2 IN a large bowl, beat eggs until frothy. Add the sour cream, vanilla extract, water, and food coloring to the bowl, beating to combine.

3 IN another bowl, mix the Almond Flour, sugar substitute, cocoa powder, and baking powder.

4 BEAT the dry ingredients into the wet ingredients, until all is combined.

5 POUR the finished batter into the prepared muffin cups, filling each cup only ⅔ of the way full. Bake 30–35 minutes, or until the centers are firm and springy, and a toothpick inserted into a cupcake comes out mostly clean.

6 LET cool 30 minutes before frosting with the Buttercream Cheese Frosting.

HELPFUL TIPS

The food coloring can be omitted but with obvious consequences—those being that these won't be "Red" Velvet Cupcakes.

CHOCOLATE LAVA CAKES
Real Chocolate Soufflés, Real Simple

These "flourless" and no-sugar-added cakes are made exactly the way I used to make soufflés in restaurant kitchens. While the thought of making a soufflé may sound daunting, I've never had one that didn't taste great, regardless of how high it rose!

SHOPPING LIST

1 tablespoon butter

1 tablespoon unsweetened cocoa powder

1 tablespoon sugar substitute

1 batch Chocolate Ganache (page 20)

2 large eggs

2 large egg yolks

¼ cup sugar substitute

½ teaspoon vanilla extract

2 tablespoons Almond Flour (page 14)

Calories: 190
Fat: 16.5g
Protein: 6.5g
Fiber: 1.5g
Net Carbs: 4.5g

Top with raspberries for the perfect garnish!

1 PREHEAT oven to 400°, and use the butter to grease the inside of four 4-ounce ramekins or small soufflé dishes.

2 COMBINE the cocoa powder with 1 tablespoon of sugar substitute. Sprinkle the mix evenly over the inside of the buttered ramekins. Refrigerate until ready to fill.

3 PREPARE the Chocolate Ganache.

4 ADD the eggs, egg yolks, sugar substitute, and vanilla extract to a bowl, and beat until frothy.

5 WHILE the Chocolate Ganache is still warm, slowly stir it into the beaten eggs until well mixed. Add the Almond Flour and mix again.

6 POUR the batter evenly between the 4 chilled ramekins, and bake for 10–12 minutes, or until springy around the edges, but still a bit soft in the center. To serve, loosen the edges of the cakes with a knife, and flip onto a plate to release.

HELPFUL TIPS

When filling the prepared ramekins, be careful not to spill any batter on the edges, as that may prevent rising.

CHOCOLATE PECAN CAKE

WITH CHOCOLATE FROSTING AND EVEN MORE PECANS

This cake is a chocolate-lover's dream, with a moist chocolate cake made without any flour and a chocolate variation on my Buttercream Cheese Frosting. Pecans add great visual appeal, flavor, and crunch.

SHOPPING LIST

Nonstick cooking spray

5 large eggs

¼ cup water

1 tablespoon vanilla extract

2½ cups Almond Flour (page 14)

¾ cup sugar substitute

¼ cup unsweetened cocoa powder

1 tablespoon baking powder

¼ cup finely chopped pecans

1 batch Buttercream Cheese Frosting (page 23)

3 tablespoons unsweetened cocoa powder

1 cup chopped pecans

Calories: 360
Fat: 34g
Protein: 12g
Fiber: 5g
Net Carbs: 5g

HELPFUL TIPS

You can make this easier by skipping the slicing in half, and making a simple 1-layer cake.

1 PLACE oven rack in the center position, and preheat to 350°. Heavily spray an 8-inch round cake pan with nonstick cooking spray.

2 IN a large bowl, beat the eggs until frothy. Add water and vanilla extract, and whisk to combine.

3 IN a medium bowl, mix the Almond Flour, sugar substitute, ¼ cup cocoa powder, and baking powder. Whisk the dry ingredients into the wet ingredients until all is combined. Fold in finely chopped pecans.

4 POUR the finished batter into the prepared cake pan, and bake 30–35 minutes, or until center is firm and spongy.

5 COOL on a wire rack for 30 minutes before refrigerating for at least 2 hours. Turn pan upside down and shake to release cake.

6 MEANWHILE, prepare the Buttercream Cheese Frosting, and fold in the 3 tablespoons of cocoa powder.

7 USING a long and thin knife, cut the cake in half horizontally to make 2 layers. Frost the bottom layer, then place the top layer over top. Frost the entire cake, and finish by pressing the cup of chopped pecans into the frosting. Cut into 12 slices to serve.

Omit the pecans and you have a classic chocolate cake!

About the Author

George Stella has been a professional chef for over thirty years. He has appeared on numerous television and news shows, including two seasons of his own show, *Low Carb and Lovin' It*, on the Food Network. Most recently he appeared on *The Dr. Oz Show* for a profile on the comfort foods the Stella family reinvented using unique and low-carb alternatives to white flour and sugar.

Connecticut born, George has spent more than half of his life in Florida, where he lives today with his wife Rachel. This is his sixth cookbook.

To keep up to date on George, please visit:

      www.StellaStyle.com

About the Photography

The food photographs and design of this book were done by **Christian and Elise Stella**, George's son and daughter-in-law. They have worked previously on the design and photography of over more than fifteen cookbooks. They are frequent collaborators with Bob Warden and did the design, photography, and co-authored his best-selling cookbook *Great Food Fast*.

All food in the photographs was purchased at an ordinary grocery store or grown in Rachel's garden and prepared to the recipe's directions. No artificial food-styling techniques were used to "enhance" the food's appearance.

RECIPE INDEX

SIDES

SNACKS

SWEET BITES

DESSERTS

mixed berry muffins 29
sausage & egg cups 30
coconut flapjacks 41
5 spice chicken salad 60
cheesy turkey burgers 61
spinach quiche 63
garlic chicken wings 69
swedish turkey meatballs 94
parmesan crusted chicken 102
roast beef 120
broiled steak 124
cheddar cheese crisps 176